MW00949215

CHANGING THE GAME

with *Casey Stoney*

FANTASTIC FEMALE FOOTBALLERS

I would like to dedicate this book to Teddy, Tilly and Willow.
You motivate me every single day to try to become
a better manager and an even better person.
Never let anyone tell you "you can't". Dream big!

A STUDIO PRESS BOOK

First published in the UK in 2019 by Studio Press,
an imprint of Bonnier Books UK,
The Plaza, 535 King's Road, London SW10 0SZ

www.studiopressbooks.co.uk
www.bonnierbooks.co.uk

© 2019 Studio Press Books

Illustration © 2019 Violet Tobacco
Text and design © 2019 Studio Press Books

1 3 5 7 9 10 8 6 4 2

All rights reserved
ISBN 978-1-78741-567-6

Written by Emily Stead
Edited by Sophie Blackman
Designed by Rob Ward

A CIP catalogue for this book is available from the British Library.
Printed and bound in Turkey

Please note: every effort has been made to ensure that the information in this
book was correct at the time it went to press. Any subsequent player,
manager or team changes are beyond the control of the publisher.

Photo credits: 10–14 (red stars) Julia August / Shutterstock; 16 John B Hewitt / Shutterstock;
60 Keeton Gale / Shutterstock; 73 Romain Biard / Shutterstock; 76 katatonia82 / Shutterstock;
82 Leonard Zhukovsky / Shutterstock; 91 Tony Feder / Stringer / Getty Images;
95 Romain Biard / Shutterstock; 109 Oleksandr Osipov / Shutterstock.

CHANGING THE GAME

with *Casey Stoney*

FANTASTIC FEMALE FOOTBALLERS

CONTENTS

INTRODUCTION

"These are the trailblazers, the pioneers, the brave. Women who have been fighting stereotypes and prejudice since the first time they kicked a football, just to play the game they love. These are the game-changers of women's football."

Having been involved in women's football for 25 years, as both a player and a coach, I've seen the game change enormously. Growing up, like many of my peers, I was told that girls couldn't – and shouldn't – play football, which only made me more determined to prove those people wrong. It's a good job I was stubborn.

I've been honoured to play for and captain some of the top clubs in England, playing alongside some amazing players. Together, we've won silverware and created memories that will last a lifetime. I've won 130 caps for my country, played in three World Cups and was the captain of Team GB at the London 2012 Olympic Games. But like the journey of so many talented sportswomen, it hasn't been easy; training without pay, in poor facilities, often without kit and even having to pay to play. I only turned professional when I was 30; until then I'd had to juggle a full-time job alongside playing and coaching, which I've done since I was 17.

While more women and girls are playing football than ever before, and perceptions of the game around the world are slowly changing, it is clear that there is still a long way to go until the playing field for men and women is level. Women in football – and in sport generally – across the globe continue to face serious challenges: they receive fewer opportunities, less investment and even today still experience discrimination playing the game they love.

An example of the pay gap at the very highest level was at the 2018 World Cup in Russia. Here, the prize money totalled $400m (£312m) for the men's tournament, while the prize fund at the Women's World Cup France 2019 was a much more modest $30m (£23.4m). Although the women's prize fund had doubled since the previous women's tournament in 2015, the goal of equality for all players, regardless of their gender, is still light years away.

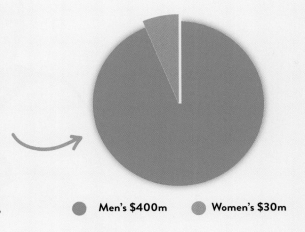

Men's $400m   Women's $30m

I'm a strong believer that football can empower women and girls and truly be the vehicle to help transform lives, and I'm thankful for all the inspirational women who have paved the way for future generations to play the game, from the players, coaches, journalists and others. This book is a celebration of just some of those fantastic women. Read about how Marta's skills saved her from poverty to conquer the world, or how Kristine Lilly smashed the world record for the number of international caps of any player, male or female. These are stories that will help you believe that dreams can come true, against all the odds.

Supporters, too, have a very important role in helping to change the game. We need a greater number of fans attending women's games to create the atmosphere and engagement that will lead to more publicity and media coverage. The more tickets and kits that are sold, the more funds that are available to invest back into the women's game. So, if you really want to change the game, then get engaged. Be it Arsenal, Manchester United or Yeovil Town, it is *your* club – both male and female – so show your support!

Casey Stoney, MBE

CASEY STONEY

A CAREER IN FOOTBALL

Born in Basildon, England, on 13 May.	**1982**
	1994 Joins Chelsea Ladies as an academy player, age 12.
Makes her senior debut for Arsenal Ladies, going on to win the league title with the Gunners twice.	**1999**
	2003 Captains England for the first time against Italy.
Leads Charlton Athletic Ladies to victory in the Premier League Cup (2004 and 2006) and the FA Women's Cup (2005).	**2004**
	2007 Signs for Chelsea Ladies.
	2007 Plays every minute of every match in the 2007 Women's World Cup as England reach the quarter-finals. Is awarded the FA International Player of the Year Award.
Reaches the final of the UEFA Women's Euro 2009 with England.	**2009**
Becomes Chelsea's player-manager in February.	**2009**
	2011 Signs for Lincoln Ladies and begins training as a full-time footballer.
Reaches the 2011 Women's World Cup quarter-finals with England.	**2011**
	2012 Is given the England captain's armband permanently by Hope Powell.
Skippers the Great Britain Olympic team at London 2012.	**2012**
	2014 Signs for Arsenal Ladies, winning the FA Women's Cup that year.
Plays in her third Women's World Cup in Canada, as England reach the semi-finals and finish third – their best-ever performance.	**2015**
	2016 Signs for Liverpool Ladies.
	2017 Plays her final international match for the Lionesses.
Retires from playing to become assistant manager of England in February.	**2018**
	2018 Appointed head coach of Manchester United Women, playing in the FA Women's Championship in June.
Manchester United WFC crowned champions for the 2018–19 season. Promoted to the Women's Super League (WSL).	**2019**

A TIMELINE OF

1894

Pioneer Nettie Honeyball placed newspaper adverts to recruit women to the British Ladies Football Club. About 30 young women joined.

1895

The first women's football match is played in England. North London beat South London 7–1.

1914

The First World War breaks out. The role of women in society changes dramatically in the UK. Women replace men who are fighting overseas – in offices, working the land and in munitions factories.

1916

The British government encourages women working in factories to play football – for their health, to boost morale and to raise money for wartime charities.

WHAT A GAME!

1920

April: The first unofficial international women's game takes place. Dick, Kerr Ladies FC from Preston beat a French XI 2–0. The attendance is 25,000.

WOMEN'S FOOTBALL

1921 The FA in England bans women from playing on Football League grounds, deeming football 'quite unsuitable for females'.

WOMEN AND FOOTBALL

The council of Football Association has prohibited the use of its grounds by women's teams, and has expressed its strong opinion that the game of football is quite unsuitable for women.

1950 The US establishes its first women's league, as four teams compete in the Craig Club Girls' Soccer League.

1920 December: On Boxing Day, 53,000 watch Dick, Kerr Ladies FC beat St Helen's Ladies 4–0. It's the biggest crowd to date for a women's game.

1969 The Women's Football Association (WFA) is formed, with 44 member clubs in England.

1971 The FA Council in England lifts the ban that denied women playing on the grounds of affiliated clubs.

STAR PLAYERS:
Lily Parr, Florrie Redford

1999
The US Women's team beat China in a penalty shoot-out to win the FIFA Women's World Cup. The final is watched by over 90,000 fans at the Rose Bowl stadium in Pasadena, CA.

STAR PLAYERS:
Michelle Akers,
Mia Hamm, Kristine Lilly

1972
A civil rights law is passed in the United States to give women equal opportunities in education, resulting in more girls playing sport at school. 'Soccer' is one of the main team sports offered to schoolgirls.

1996
Women's football is contested for the first time at an Olympic Games, in Atlanta, GA. The final attracts a crowd of over 76,000 as the United States win gold.

1972
The first official women's international in Britain is played at Greenock. England beat Scotland 3–2.

1985
The US National Women's Soccer Team plays its first match against Italy.

1991
The first FIFA Women's World Cup, featuring 12 teams, takes place in China. The United States win the tournament.

STAR PLAYERS:
Sun Wen, Sissi,
Brandi Chastain

2001

In the US, the Women's United Soccer Association (WUSA) is the world's first women's football league in which all its players were paid as professionals. It folds in 2003, making massive losses.

2011

Japan become the first team from Asia to win the FIFA Women's World Cup.

STAR PLAYERS:
Homare Sawa,
Abby Wambach, Marta

The first Women's Super League (WSL) season kicks off in England.

STAR PLAYERS:
Rachel Yankey,
Karen Carney, Casey Stoney

2012

In January in the US, the Women's Professional Soccer League folds due to lack of finances after three seasons. It is replaced by the current National Women's Soccer League (NWSL).

STAR PLAYERS:
Christine Sinclair, Carli Lloyd

NOW

Women's football is played at a professional level around the globe, with 155 active international women's teams. While the sport continues to grow, both in participation and popularity, media coverage, pay and opportunities in women's football still have a long way to go to match those of the men's game.

STAR PLAYERS:
Ada Hegerberg,
Sam Kerr, Alex Morgan

2012

England reach the quarter-finals of the London 2012 Olympics, as the United States win gold again. Some 80,000 fans watch the final in August at Wembley Stadium.

LILY PARR

BLAZING A TRAIL

Dick, Kerr Ladies FC were a trailblazing team that formed at a munitions factory in England during the First World War.

Seen as one of the most important teams in the history of women's football, the skilful side from Preston in northwest England played between 1917 and 1965. Lily Parr played in the outside-left position and was the star of the side, scoring more than 900 goals.

A CURIOUS CHILDHOOD

Lily was born in St Helens, Lancashire, the fourth of seven children. Growing up, she showed little interest in traditional girls' hobbies such as sewing and cooking. Instead, her strong physique allowed her to compete with boys on the football and rugby fields. She often played football on waste ground with her brothers, who encouraged her.

She began playing competitively during the war, joining St Helens Ladies in 1919. Lily's talents were quickly spotted and she was given a job in the Dick, Kerr and Company factory, Preston, where she played for the ladies' team and was paid expenses of 10 shillings per match (£15 or $18 today). In her first season, aged 14, Lily scored 43 goals. Her shots were said to be harder than any male rival's.

PRESTON'S PIONEER

Tall and powerful, Lily was an aggressive player with great technical ability. She was known for scoring from extraordinary angles with some rocketing left-foot strikes, all while playing with a heavy leather ball. Her teammate Joan Whalley feared being on the end of Lily's crosses, as she had a 'kick like a mule'. One shot was rumoured to have broken a male goalkeeper's arm!

Neither her chain-smoking habit nor her huge appetite appeared to hinder Lily's performances during a thirty-year football career. In 1946, the fearsome forward was made Preston Ladies' captain in recognition of her 26 years' service, having missed only five games since joining.

The local newspaper reported that she had scored 967 goals during this time – an astonishing record for a player of any gender in any era. She ended her playing days in 1951.

FORWARD

STATS

Country .... England

Club .... Dick, Kerr Ladies FC

Born .... 26 April 1905

Died .... 22 May 1978

Height .... 1.78 m

A LEAGUE OF THEIR OWN

During the war, women volunteers took over the roles of men who were fighting overseas. Many of these women became factory 'munitionettes', working long hours in hazardous conditions to produce ammunition for the war effort. The British government encouraged women to play football for their physical wellbeing and to boost morale.

The Dick, Kerr Ladies team was established in 1917 and quickly became popular, thanks to their fearless and skilled displays. Fans flocked to watch the side and support grew from a few thousand fans to 53,000 in a match against St Helens on Boxing Day, 1920. A further 14,000 people waited without tickets outside the ground! It was a world-record crowd for a women's club fixture that would stand for 98 years. The match raised over £3,000 (more than £97,000 in today's money) for charities.

STRONG OPPOSITION

The Dick, Kerr Ladies went from strength to strength on the pitch, but not everyone was willing to celebrate the team's success. As Britain began to recover from war, the factories closed and women were demoted to roles in the home, which was deemed their 'right and proper place' in society. Football's health benefits were no longer championed, and the game was now considered to be 'most unsuitable... for a woman's physical frame'.

KEY SKILLS

INCREDIBLE POWER

GLORIOUS GOALS RECORD

TOP TECHNIQUE

CASEY'S LOWDOWN

"A real history-maker who performed in front of crowds that women's teams today can only dream of."

MEMORIALS

A casting of Lily Parr on the Football Walk of Fame outside the National Football Museum in Manchester recognizes the feats of the first world-class women's footballer.

Over 30 million women and girls play football worldwide, with 4.8 million registered players in 2014.

Many middle-class members of the English Football Association were appalled that women's teams had raised money through ticket sales for the families of working-class miners, and began a propaganda campaign to end the golden age of women's football. In 1921 the FA banned women's matches from being played in their grounds. The ban lasted for 50 years and changed the course of women's football forever.

Despite the ban, Dick, Kerr Ladies continued to play, and in 1922 they toured to North America. Forbidden from playing in Canada, they headed to America, taking on – and beating – men's sides in front of crowds of up to 10,000 spectators.

In 1926, the team lost the support of the owners of the Dick, Kerr and Company factory and changed their name to Preston Ladies FC. However, the team carried on, and eventually disbanded in 1965 due to a lack of players – just four years before the Women's Football Association was formed.

A LEGEND'S LEGACY

In 2002 Lily became the first female to be inducted into English football's Hall of Fame at the National Football Museum. A role model for women and girls everywhere, this pioneer of the women's game has since been joined by 16 more female footballers.

Lily is also remembered as a gay icon. She met her partner, Mary, while training as a nurse at Whittingham Hospital, Preston, aged 18. Although attitudes towards same-sex relationships were only just becoming socially acceptable, they lived together until Lily's death in 1978. The Lily Parr Exhibition Trophy, a lesbian football event, was played in 2007 and 2009 in honour of a legend who paved the way for future generations to play the game she loved.

Played for
ST HELENS
LADIES
1919

Played for
DICK, KERR
LADIES
1920–1926

Played for
PRESTON
LADIES
1926–1951

BELLA REAY

SPARTAN COURAGE

Bella Reay was another munitions worker who excelled on the football field during the First World War. Born Isabella Reay in 1900, Bella was the daughter of a coal miner. She worked in the South Docks of Blyth, Northumberland, in the northeast of England, helping to load ships with fresh ammunition.

Bella and her fellow workers played football on the nearby beach during their breaks, sometimes coached by Royal Navy sailors whose ship was stationed in the harbour. In July 1917, the workers formed an official team, supported by Blyth Spartans FC, who donated green-and-white-striped shirts to the ladies.

REAY OF LIGHT

Blyth Spartan Ladies, led by Reay, quickly became an exceptional team, winning 26 and drawing four of the matches on their way to winning the Munitionettes' Cup in 1918. Large crowds came to watch the matches, with the profits donated to wartime charities.

CASEY'S LOWDOWN

"Bella had an unbelievable goals record and must have been a nightmare to mark! Playing on poor-quality pitches makes her goals record all the more impressive."

Bella's only football trophy was won on 18 May 1918. In front of 22,000 supporters at Ayresome Park, Blyth Spartans Ladies beat Bolckow Vaughan 5–0 in a replayed final to clinch the Munitionettes' Cup. Reay scored a hat-trick, and her teammate Jennie Morgan, who came straight from her wedding ceremony, added two more goals. The team was greeted in Blyth with a heroes' welcome.

FORWARD

STATS

Country .... England
Club .... Blyth Spartans AFC
Born 1900
Died 1979

The unbeaten Blyth Spartans Ladies folded in 1919. Reay married in 1920, becoming Mrs Bella Henstock, and had two daughters. She continued to work in the shipyards and played football in friendly matches and fundraisers.

Reay's story is just one of many pioneering female footballers' histories that is rarely told. We know that 17-year-old Bella was a quick centre-forward who scored a phenomenal 133 goals in a season. Reay remains an inspiration to many in Blyth and beyond.

HEGE RIISE

NORWAY'S FINEST

Attacking midfielder Hege Riise is regularly hailed as the best player in Norway's history. She had an outstanding career, winning a trio of top prizes – the FIFA Women's World Cup, the UEFA Women's Championship and an Olympic gold medal.

By the time Hege retired from international duty in 2004, she had broken the record for the most-capped player for her country – a record that stands today. Now a manager, Riise works with the same passion for the game as she displayed during her playing days.

LOVE OF THE GAME

Born in Lørenskog on the outskirts of Norway's capital city, Oslo, Hege enjoyed playing sport from a young age. She began playing football alongside skiing and handball, but it was football that captured young Hege's heart.

Hege joined a boys' team at the age of six and played football before and after school. She loved the game, but as the only girl, her teammates and opponents were often stronger and faster than she was. Hege quickly learned to be creative with the ball and worked on her strength and pace to keep up with the boys. There were few opportunities for girls to play football in Lørenskog, and it wasn't until Hege was 14 that she at last found a girls' side. It was then that she really focused on football, and her reputation as a hardworking and creative player grew. At first, Hege found it hard to imagine herself playing at the highest level,

RIISE
6

FORWARD

STATS

Country	Norway
Born	18 July 1969
Height	1.65 m
International caps	188
International goals	58

though her confidence would later soar. She began her club career with local side Setskog-Høland, and won the Norwegian cup in 1992, her first piece of silverware.

RIISE TO THE TOP

It wasn't until she was in her late teens that Hege discovered Norway had a women's national team! She was 20 when she made her international debut in 1990, as the team entered its most successful period. The following year, Hege helped her country reach the final of the first FIFA Women's World Cup, held in China. Norway made it all the way to the final, which was attended by an incredible 63,000 fans, but narrowly lost to the US.

Honours followed in 1993 as Norway won the UEFA Women's Championship. They beat hosts Italy to be crowned champions.

> # "The strongest element of my game was seeing situations that other players didn't see."
>
> ### *HEGE RIISE*

Two years later, Norway arrived at the 1995 World Cup with confidence. At 25, Riise was at the top of her game. She was instrumental in helping Norway win its first World Cup, scoring five goals, including a stunning opener in the final against Germany. Her skilful performances in midfield saw Hege win the Golden Ball, awarded to the best player in the tournament.

Riise won a third major trophy with Norway at the 2000 Olympic Games in Sydney. After losing to the United States in the first group match, the teams met again in the gold-medal play-off. This time, Norway triumphed, winning 3–2, after a late US equalizer took the match to extra time. As Norway claimed the gold, Riise became one of three women in the world to have won the top prize at the Olympics, the World Cup and the European Championship.

At the end of the 2006 season, Hege retired a legend, aged 36. Her 188 international caps set a record for all Norwegian footballers, male and female. It will take some beating.

ADVENTURES ABROAD

Following World Cup glory in 1995, Hege moved from Setskog-Høland to play in Japan alongside her Norway teammate Linda Medalen. The pair joined the Nikko Shoken Dream Ladies, winning back-to-back

Played for
SETSKOG-
HØLAND
1991–95
Trophies:
1 x Norwegian Cup

**2003
UEFA Women's
Championship:
Winner**

**1995 FIFA
Women's World
Cup: Winner &
Golden Ball**

Played for
NIKKO SHOKEN
DREAM LADIES
1996–97
Trophies:
*2 x Japanese Leagues,
2 x Japanese Cups*

**1996
Atlanta
Olympic
Games:
Bronze
medal**

Played for
SETSKOG-
HØLAND
1998–99

Japanese league titles and two Japanese cups before the club ran into financial troubles. Hege honed her skills during two enjoyable seasons in Japan before returning home for a second spell with Setskog-Høland.

Another move followed in 2001, as Carolina Courage in North Carolina asked Hege to play in the US's Premier League, WUSA. The players were adored by large crowds and Riise felt honoured to become a role model.

MOVE INTO MANAGEMENT

When the time to hang up her boots drew near, Hege became player-manager at Team Strømmen, a club in Norway's Toppserien division. She became head coach in 2006, and in 2008 took the team close to glory, as they finished as runners-up in the league and cup. In 2017, LSK Kvinner offered Hege the manager's job. There, she coaches using her outstanding ability to read the play. Her vision

of the game is famous and as a player she was once called 'the woman with six pairs of eyes'.

Riise recognizes that women's football is decades behind the men's game and is not afraid to tackle these issues. She dreams of being able to train a team with enough resources to help each player reach her potential, paying an annual salary that would allow her team enough rest time. Might Riise one day manage Norway's national side? Watch this space.

CASEY'S LOWDOWN

"One of the first women I remember watching, Hege read the game brilliantly. She contributed a huge amount to Norway's dominant decade."

Played for
ASKER FK
2000
Trophies:
1 x Norwegian Cup

2000 Sydney Olympic Games: Gold Medal

First woman to receive Norway's Golden Ball in 2004

Played for
CAROLINA COURAGE
2001–04
Trophies:
WUSA Founders Cup 2002

Played for
TEAM STRØMMEN
2005–06

SUN WEN

CHINA'S FINEST

Probably the finest forward that Asia has produced, Sun Wen is an exceptional talent who led by example. The striker played for China in four World Cups and at two Olympic Games, captaining her side during China's golden age of football.

Sun Wen was a big match player like no other, with a determined will to win. When games were at stalemate, Sun Wen could always be relied upon to get on the score sheet or conjure up an assist for her teammates.

STAR OF SHANGHAI

Born in 1973 in Shanghai, Sun Wen began playing football at the age of eight at a local sports school. She loved the game and often watched matches in the Chinese men's league with her father at a time when football was far from fashionable. In the 1980s, the Chinese football authorities set out on an ambitious journey to modernize the game. The national women's team, nicknamed the Steel Roses, played their first international match in 1986.

During her teenage years, Sun Wen's progression was swift. She began playing for local club Shanghai in 1989, and used her slender frame to slip past defenders and provide a deadly finish. Sun was picked for the national team when she had just turned 17. She would become an important player.

WORLD CUP MEMORIES

Sun Wen made one of her greatest football memories when she played in the first FIFA Women's World Cup in her home country in 1991. The stadium in Guangzhou was packed with a staggering 65,000 fans for China's opening match – unheard of for a women's football match. The atmosphere was electric. As the national anthem played before the teams kicked off, 18-year-old Wen could barely contain her nerves. The game finished 4–0 to the hosts, as the Chinese crowd went wild. China went on to reach the quarter-finals.

Four years later, at the 1995 World Cup in Sweden, the Steel Roses progressed to the semis before suffering a narrow penalty shoot-out defeat to hosts US in the iconic 1999 final. Sun Wen's third World Cup was

SUN W
9

MIDFIELDER

STATS

Country	China
Born	6 April 1973
Height	1.62 m
International caps	152
International goals	106

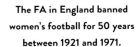

The FA in England banned women's football for 50 years between 1921 and 1971.

to be her greatest. Her storming displays and seven goals earned her both the Golden Ball and Golden Shoe trophies (the latter award was shared with Brazil's Sissi) for the best player and top scorer in the tournament.

An exceptional captain, Wen also led her team to an Olympic Silver medal at the Atlanta Olympics in 1996, where women's football was contested for the first time. Over four World Cups and two Olympic Games, Sun Wen did not miss a single minute of play. Her 16 goals in 28 games confirm just how key a player she was.

Sadly, the weight of responsibility took its toll on Sun Wen's body, and she was forced to take a two-year absence from the national side when she was 30. The same knee injury ended her international career in 2006, by which time Wen had won over 150 caps. Her last act with China was winning a sixth AFC Women's Asian Cup.

IMPOSSIBLE MISSION?

As well as being a talented football journalist and FIFA ambassador, Wen now works with youth players in Shanghai, and is keen to pass on her footballing knowledge and love for the game to the next generation.

Her task has been far from easy. While the numbers of girls participating in football in China is increasing each year, players often encounter discrimination, body-shaming or they simply cannot afford to play the game outside of school at expensive clubs.

Since Sun Wen's playing days, progress in the women's game has been slow. However, the Chinese Football Association (CFA) recently announced fresh plans to develop the women's game, by building from grassroots level – allocating funds to school and university leagues, as in the US.

Played for
SHANGHAI
1989–2000

AFC Women's Asian Cup: Winner 1991, 1993, 1995, 1997, 1999, 2006

1996 Atlanta Olympic Games: Silver Medal

1999 FIFA Women's World Cup: Runner-up

AFC Women's Footballer of the Year: 1999

Top Chinese men's clubs will also be required to establish women's teams by 2020, which can only be good news for women's football in China.

If among the next generation another Sun Wen is discovered, the CFA will be satisfied. But the former forward's goals are more modest – if girls are allowed the freedom to play the game they love, her mission will be complete.

CASEY'S LOWDOWN

"Wen's goals-to-games ratio for China is one of the best ever in the women's game. Her movement and clinical finishing should be studied by all young forwards."

"The 1999 World Cup was a great experience in my life, even now I feel like it was a dream. The result didn't matter – what was important is that we pushed women's football to a higher level."

SUN WEN

1999 FIFA Women's World Cup: Golden Ball & Golden Shoe, (joint with Sissi)

Played for
ATLANTA BEAT
2001–02

FIFA Female Player of the Century – voted 2002 – (joint with Michelle Akers)

Played for
SHANGHAI SVA
2003, 2006
Teammates:
Homare Sawa, Briana Scurry

MICHELLE AKERS

ALL-AMERICAN GIRL

Michelle was born in Santa Clara, California, in 1966, though she spent much of her childhood in Seattle. There she dreamed of playing American Football for the NFL's Pittsburgh Steelers, only to be told by her elementary school teacher that 'girls don't play football'.

Instead, Akers took up the more acceptable game of soccer, playing against boys in her local neighbourhood. Girls growing up in Akers' generation were not 'supposed' to sweat, get dirty or even be assertive, but she shunned the remarks and the glares to follow her sporting dream.

While at high school in Seattle, Michelle was honoured as a three-time 'All-American' for her skilled displays. A sports scholarship to the University of Central Florida (UFC) followed, a period that saw Michelle selected four times as an All-American, and she become the all-time leading scorer in the university's history. She was so exceptional that her number 10 shirt was retired by UCF. Michelle set the style of play that would serve her well during her career – she was physical and aggressive, which made her almost impossible to stop. By the time she graduated, she stood at 5 foot 10 inches tall.

NATURAL GOALSCORER

On 18 August 1985, while still a teenager, Michelle was selected for the United States women's national team in the squad's first international match. While injury kept her out of the match against Italy, her first appearance would follow just days later against Denmark. She marked her debut with a goal, which was also the team's first goal in their history. Akers used her long stride to power past defenders and unleash lethal shots, scoring 15 goals in 24 games for the United States between 1985 and 1990, and setting an astonishing team record 39 goals in 26 games in a single season in 1991.

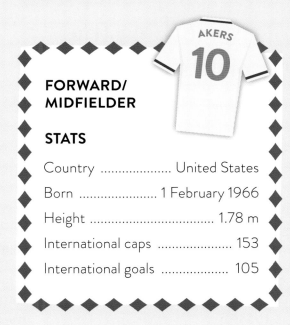

FORWARD/ MIDFIELDER

STATS

Country .... United States

Born .... 1 February 1966

Height .... 1.78 m

International caps 153

International goals 105

In 1991, the United States team travelled to China to compete in the first Women's World Cup. Michelle thrived on the world stage and had the tournament of her life, scoring five goals in the quarter-finals and 10 altogether to win the Golden Shoe.

> "The challenge is to take difficult and painful times and turn them into something beneficial, something that makes you grow."

MICHELLE AKERS

A record crowd in the stadium saw Michelle score twice in the final as the United States edged out Norway to become World Champions for the first time. Despite this momentous victory, there was no live broadcast of the final back in the United States.

CHANGE OF ROLE

As Michelle entered her late twenties, each game was proving more exhausting. It took the tough striker longer to recover between games, too. Sadly, Michelle was forced to give up her place when she was diagnosed with chronic fatigue and immune dysfunction syndrome in 1994. She tailored her diet and training to allow her to continue playing, and took up a new role as a defensive midfielder, with the aim of avoiding some of the punishing tackles she had received as a striker. Although

United States Soccer Federation (USSF) Female Athlete of the Year: 1990, 1991

Played for
TYRESÖ FF
1990, 1992, 1994

Teammate:
Kristine Lilly

1991 FIFA Women's World Cup: Winner & Golden Shoe

1991 FIFA Women's World Cup: Silver Ball

Played for
ORLANDO LIONS WOMEN

1992

she missed the buzz of scoring, she made the new position her own. The following year, her 1995 World Cup ended early, when Akers suffered a concussion and a knee injury. This time, Norway had their revenge, eliminating the US in the semi-final.

More glory followed for the United States as the team won the gold medal at the 1996 Olympic Games in Atlanta, along with a second World Cup in 1999. Michelle retired from the game just before the 2000 Sydney Olympics. Since then she has continued to act as a fierce advocate for women's football in the United States.

Michelle feels blessed to have had such a fantastic career, but we can only wonder how many goals she may have gone on to score had she not been struck down by illness. She was inducted into the National Soccer Hall of Fame in Texas in 2004, and remains a legend of the women's game.

CASEY'S LOWDOWN

"A true pioneer of the women's game, Michelle was an incredible athlete and competitor for the United States."

1996 Atlanta Olympic Games: Gold Medal

1998 FIFA Order of Merit

1999 FIFA Women's World Cup: Winner

2002 FIFA Female Player of the Century (joint with Sun Wen)

KRISTINE LILLY

LEADING LIGHT

Kristine Lilly was born in Connecticut in 1971. She is celebrated in the US for being the most-capped player in the game (male or female), playing an unbelievable 354 times over 23 years and four different decades for her country. Her caps record may never be broken.

Capable of playing in any attacking role, Kristine also chipped in with an impressive 130 goals for the US, and sits third in the table of her country's leading goalscorers. She played on two World Cup-winning sides – 1991 and 1999 – and can boast two Olympic gold medals and a silver in her collection. Despite wearing the number 13 jersey throughout her career, the luck appeared to always be with the long-serving Lilly.

SERIOUS ABOUT SOCCER

Kristine, a prodigious talent with an eye for a goal, was recruited to the national side early – she was still at high school when her first call-up came in 1987. The United States' women's team had been formed just two years earlier and had grand ambitions for its senior side. She went on to study at the University of North Carolina, starring for the North Carolina Tar Heels college team.

Serious about playing at the highest level, Kristine followed in the footsteps of her US teammate, Michelle Akers, by moving overseas to join Tyresö FF, a club that competed in the Swedish Championship. She stayed for a season before returning to the US with the Washington Warthogs. Playing in an indoor soccer league, she held her own as the only woman in the whole division.

LILLY
13

FORWARD/ MIDFIELDER

STATS

Country .... United States

Born .... 22 July 1971

Height .... 1.63 m

International caps 354

International goals 130

Then in 2001, the world's first women's professional league (WUSA) in which all players were paid was established. Kristine captained the Boston Breakers, playing every minute of every match for her team in the league's first season. Kristine was thrilled to be playing the game she loved for a living, but the league ran into financial troubles and folded in 2004. The Breakers' head coach, former Swedish legend Pia Sundage, offered Kristine a lifeline, and in 2005 the pair signed for KIF Örebro DFF in Sweden.

33

In 2008 Kristine took some time off from football, as her first child, Sidney, was born. But even at 37, the famous forward still had much to offer and was not ready to retire. She returned for a second spell with the Boston Breakers when a new professional league, the Women's Professional Soccer league (WPS), was formed. In the 2009 season, the attacker was ever-present for her side and played for the side until her retirement in 2011.

LILLY THE LEGEND

Kristine's international career was nothing less than extraordinary. She played in five World Cups between 1991 and 2007, twice winning the title, and medalled at three Olympic Games.

A further gold medal at the 2008 Games in Sydney would undoubtedly have belonged to Lilly, had the tournament not fallen so

close to the birth of her eldest daughter. Just five months after becoming a mother, Kristine was lining up for the US again.

Many Americans best remember Kristine for her crucial headed clearance off the goal-line in extra time of the 1999 Women's World Cup final. She then scored in the penalty shoot-out that followed to clinch the trophy for the United States. Ever-hungry for success, Kristine decided not to retire alongside her teammates

CASEY'S LOWDOWN

"When I first played against Kristine, I quickly realized how good she was. A natural goalscorer and one of the fittest players in the women's game, too."

1991 FIFA Women's World Cup: Winner

US Soccer Player of the Year: Winner 1993, 2005, 2006

Played for TYRESÖ FF *1994*

Teammate:
Michelle Akers

WASHINGTON WARTHOGS (indoors) *1995*

1996 Atlanta Olympic Games: Gold Medal

Mia Hamm, Joy Fawcett and Julie Foudy, following the team's 'farewell tour' in 2004. Some of her career highlights were yet to follow. Two years later, she finished second in the voting for FIFA's Women's World Player of the Year award, and earned her 300th international cap. Her final cap – number 354 – was in 2010. To explain just how astounding a feat this was, football's second-most-capped player, Egypt's Ahmed Hassan, has 184 caps.

After retirement, Kristine became a youth coach, and now combines running the Kristine Lilly Soccer Academy with her role as an ambassador for the US Soccer Foundation.

Member of the US Women's National All-Time Best XI Team

> "Scoring your first goal makes you feel like you belong. Scoring your last goal makes you feel like you still belong."

KRISTINE LILLY

DELAWARE GENIES
1998

1999 FIFA Women's World Cup: Winner

2000 Sydney Olympic Games: Silver Medal

BOSTON BREAKERS
2001–03, 2009–11

2004 Athens Olympic Games: Gold Medal

Captain of the US team: 2005–2007

An international record of caps: 354

KIF ÖREBRO DFF
2005

Teammate: Christie Welsh

KELLY SMITH

WORLD CLASS

Kelly Smith was a truly talented number 10, and is considered by fans, coaches and her fellow players alike to be the finest female footballer that England has ever produced.

Kelly had to overcome many obstacles during her career, but the highs outweighed the lows as she retired from the game with a host of trophies and individual honours. Her creativity, passing skills and spectacular goals have inspired many young girls to take up the game, both in the United States and back home in England.

CHILDHOOD DREAM

Born and brought up in Watford, Kelly had a ball at her feet from the moment she could walk. At primary school, she played football with the boys and joined the Garston Boys Club outside of school. Kelly's first setback came at the age of seven, when parents complained about boys playing against – and being outclassed by – a girl. She left the club as their leading goalscorer. Kelly refused to let this hold her back and her father formed Pinner Park, a girls' team where Kelly could compete against girls her own age. After five years, the team joined forces with Wembley Ladies and Kelly was promoted to the first team, aged 15. She made her senior debut in the 1994–95 season, juggling matches and training alongside her schoolwork.

Kelly had longed to be discovered by an Arsenal scout, and was thrilled when the

FORWARD

STATS

Country .... England
Born .... 29 October 1978
Height .... 1.68 m
International caps 117
International goals 46

chance to join Arsenal Ladies came up when she was 18. In her first season with the Gunners, the gifted forward helped the team to win the FA Women's Premier League title. Back then, however, Kelly saw football as a hobby. There was no such job as a professional women's footballer, or so she thought.

MOVE OVERSEAS

Kelly's fortunes changed when she was scouted by three American colleges. Although she was nervous about leaving home so young, she was desperate to follow her dream. Kelly accepted a scholarship with Seton Hall, where she hit 76 goals in 51 matches, attracting interest from senior clubs in the States. She later joined Philadelphia Charge in the first professional women's football league, the WUSA. A flair player, Kelly delighted crowds with her mastery of the ball and ability to dribble past players – skills that were not often on show in the direct, physical game American fans were used to. She had three seasons at Philadelphia, though spent months on the sidelines after suffering two serious knee injuries. Then, at the end of the 2003 season, the league collapsed. Kelly stayed on for the following season with the New Jersey Wildcats, but sadly a broken leg ended her time in the States. Faced with the thought that she might not ever be able to play football again, Kelly entered a dark place. She returned to England and completed a period of therapy before rejoining Arsenal for two more spells at the club. Her club career saw Kelly win five league titles, six FA Cups and the top women's prize in Europe, in 2007. That season, Arsenal won the quadruple with Kelly in outstanding form, averaging almost a goal a game.

ENGLAND'S LIONESS

As well as her impressive haul of trophies with Arsenal, Kelly was an icon for England's national side. She made her international

CASEY'S LOWDOWN

"I was privileged to train and play with Kelly for both club and country. She was one of the most technically gifted players that England has produced. She often kept her team in the game and had a wand of a left foot."

1991 FIFA Women's World Cup: Winner

Played for
WEMBLEY LADIES
1994–96

Played for
ARSENAL LADIES
1996–97, 2005–09, 2012–2017
Trophies: 5 x English League titles, 1 x UEFA Women's Cup,
6 x English League Cups, 4 x FA Premier League Cups,
2 x FA Community Shields
Teammates: Casey Stoney, Alex Scott

Played for
NEW JERSEY LADY STALLIONS
1999–2000

debut just three days after her 17th birthday, though it might have been earlier had Kelly not been sitting her exams. An automatic pick for the next 20 years, Kelly won 117 caps and scored a record 46 goals, while providing many more assists for her teammates.

She played in two World Cups, in China 2007 and Germany 2011 (injury caused her to miss the 2015 tournament), and in four European Championships. The forward's most famous goals were a crucial strike against Japan in China, and a cheeky lob from the halfway line against Russia in the Euro 2009 championships, where England finished as runners-up. Kelly also starred for Great Britain at the London 2012 Olympics, helping her team to beat Brazil in front of more than 70,000 fans at Wembley Stadium.

Having retired from playing at the age of 38, Kelly now works as a full-time coach at Arsenal, and considers her role as a fantastic

opportunity to pay back the club she loves. Having enjoyed such a stellar career, Kelly is ready to pass on the baton to the next generation of female footballing talent.

"I want to make an impact on the lives of women and girls around the world and show them that they can achieve their goals."

KELLY SMITH

Played for
PHILADELPHIA
CHARGE
2001–2003
Teammates:
Hope Solo

Played for
NEW
JERSEY
WILDCATS
2004

**Appointed
Member
of the British
Empire
(MBE):
2008**

Played for
BOSTON
BREAKERS
2009–2012
Teammates:
Alex Scott

*England
Women's
all-time record
goalscorer*

**PFA Lifetime
Achievement
Award**

BIRGIT PRINZ

WORLD BEATER

Birgit is a legend of women's football in Germany and one of the game's true greats. Her hat-trick of FIFA Women's World Player of the Year awards and two World Cups were highlights of a remarkable career in football.

From the very start of her career, Birgit had one goal: to be the best. As soon as she won a title or individual trophy, it was quickly forgotten. The striker was already targeting her next achievement. This approach won her an enormous haul of honours and a reputation as an undisputed legend of world football.

WUNDERKIND

As a young girl growing up in West Germany, Birgit excelled in a number of sports. Her father, a football coach, introduced Birgit to football at his youth club, SV Dörnigheim. She made rapid progress and signed for FSV Frankfurt in 1993 aged 15. Birgit made her debut for the Bundesliga club that same year and never looked back. A tall, hungry striker, who used her physical presence to overpower defenders, she was difficult to mark because she knew exactly when to turn on the pace to unleash a shot on goal.

In 1997 and 1998 she was the league's top scorer, which earned her a move across town to local rivals FFC Frankfurt. It was a match made in heaven! Over 13 seasons

at the club, Birgit won six Bundesliga titles and eight German cups. With Birgit leading the line, Frankfurt were a force at home and in Europe, winning three UEFA Women's Cups between 2002 and 2008.

FIRM FOCUS

While Birgit admits that she 'never wanted to save the world', preferring to concentrate on her own game than with matters off the pitch, the striker was an innovator. Throughout her playing career, Birgit would always push herself to meet the next challenge. A stint in the United States saw her win the 2002 WUSA Championship, then, following the 2003

PRINZ
9

FORWARD

STATS

Country .... Germany
Born .... 25 October 1977
Height .... 1.79 m
Club appearances 282
Club goals 282
International caps 214
International goals 128

World Cup, Birgit was offered a move to play in Italy's Serie A with the men's club, AC Perugia. The groundbreaking transfer did not go ahead as Birgit pulled out, fearing the move might have been more of a publicity stunt than a genuine interest in her game – she was definitely not a player who was happy to warm the bench!

GERMAN GIANT

Birgit played for Germany during the most successful period in their history. As a 16-year-old, she made her international debut as a substitute against Canada. It took her less than 15 minutes to mark the occasion with a goal – the first of a record-breaking 128 she would go on to score for her country. Germany's first World Cup win came in 2003, when the tournament was hosted by the United States. Birgit claimed both the Golden Ball and Golden Shoe awards for the best player and

top scorer, with seven goals. A second World Cup was won in 2007 in China, as Birgit bagged five tournament goals, including one in the final against Marta's Brazil, to secure more glory for Germany. Within European competition, Germany were unstoppable. The National Eleven won a supreme five UEFA European

CASEY'S LOWDOWN

"The best forward in the world when she was at her peak, Birgit had the ability to score many different types of goals. She was extremely strong and powerful, and one of the toughest opponents a defender could face."

Played for
FSV FRANKFURT
1993–98
Trophies:
2 x German League Titles,
2 x German Cups

UEFA
Women's
Championship:
Winner
**1995, 1997,
2001, 2005,
2009**

Bundesliga
top scorer:
**1997, 1998,
2003, 2007**

Played for
FFC FRANKFURT
1998–2002, 2003–2011
Trophies:
6 x German League Titles,
8 x German Cups,
3 x UEFA Women's Cups

**2000
Sydney
Olympic
Games:
Bronze
Medal**

Championships with Prinz playing as their number 9. Birgit retired at the age of 34, having played a record 214 times, and with a bulging trophy cabinet to rival any player in the game.

TEAM ETHIC

From the moment the towering striker scored her debut goal for Germany, Birgit was thrust into the media spotlight, which the young star never welcomed. Although Birgit's goals unsurprisingly made headlines, the striker always repeated that Germany's success was down to a team of 11 players. Off the pitch, Birgit trained as a sports psychologist, and has worked with all levels, from youth football, men's football and with the German women's senior side. As a player with an incredible will to win and strong team mentality, her influence is invaluable in helping to develop the careers of others.

> "First games are always special. It was great to be allowed to play Bundesliga at the age of 15."
>
> **BIRGIT PRINZ**

German Female Footballer of the Year: 2001–08

FIFA Women's World Player of the Year: Winner 2002, 2003, 2004

Played for
CAROLINA COURAGE
2002–03
Trophies:
1 x US League Title
Teammate: *Hege Riise*

2003 FIFA Women's World Cup: Winner, Golden Ball & Golden Shoe

2005 UEFA Women's Championship: Golden Player

2004 Athens Olympic Games: Bronze Medal

2008 Beijing Olympic Games: Bronze Medal

2007 FIFA Women's World Cup: Winner & Silver Ball

HOPE SOLO

GOLDEN GLOVES

Incredible stopper Hope Solo earned her place as the United States' number one of all time, helping her team to win two Olympic Gold medals and the 2015 FIFA Women's World Cup.

She combined excellent positioning and quick reflexes to become the first woman to keep 100 international clean sheets, rewriting many more records for the US along the way. Perhaps her most extraordinary achievement was playing 55 consecutive matches without letting in a single goal between 2002 and 2008 – the longest undefeated streak by a goalkeeper in US history. But Hope's career could have been very different...

KEEPING GOAL

Hope was born and raised in the small town of Richland, Washington. She spent her first years in football playing as a forward and loved to score goals. But when she was 15, an injury to her team's goalkeeper saw the tall, skinny teenager switch positions. She impressed, but at the time, goalkeeping was not glamorous, and Hope's heart wasn't in it. She agreed to play for the state team in goal, but the rest of the time continued to play as a forward. By the end of high school, colleges from all over the country wanted Hope to play for them – although she still wasn't sure which position was her best. She even considered focusing on a career in basketball. It was only when one of her coaches, Amy Griffin – a former World Cup goalkeeper herself – told Hope that she could be one of the best goalkeepers in the world that she was convinced to the pull on the gloves for good.

TURNING PRO

Hope spent her first professional season with the Philadelphia Charge in 2003, but the league went bust and folded at the end of the season. Swedish club Gothenburg signed Hope for the following season, before a switch to Lyon in the French league in 2005. Hope enjoyed Europe – the fans, her teammates and coaches made it a special time. By the time she returned to America, She was stronger as both a person and a player, and she became the United States first-choice goalkeeper in 2005.

SOLO
1

GOALKEEPER

STATS

Country .... United States

Born .... 30 July 1981

Height .... 1.75 m

Club appearances 134

International caps 202

"We all fall; the key is knowing how to rise."

HOPE SOLO

The 2007 World Cup in China was her first major tournament as number one and the team progressed to the semis, having conceded just two goals along the way. Disappointment was to follow when Hope was dropped for the semi-final match against Brazil, and the team lost 4–0. The match also marked the end of the team's record unbeaten run. Hope was devastated, but would come back stronger.

Two Olympic Gold medals, at Beijing 2008 and London 2012, sandwiched a penalty shoot-out World Cup defeat to Japan in 2011. It was during these tournaments that Hope showed her strength on the world stage. At the World Cup in Germany, she won the Golden Glove award for the best goalkeeper and the Bronze Ball for her overall performance.

Hope again led the United States to glory at the 2015 World Cup in neighbouring Canada, where record-breaking TV audiences topped 750 million viewers around the world. Hope was ever-present in goal, making some crucial saves on the way to the final, including a semi-final penalty save. For her outstanding play, she won her second consecutive Golden Glove Award. Hope was an American hero.

Played for
PHILADELPHIA
CHARGE
2003
Teammates:
*Kelly Smith,
Marinette Pichon*

Played for
KOPPARBERGS/
GÖTEBORG
2004

Played for
OLYMPIQUE
LYONNAIS
2005

**2008 Beijing
Olympic Games:
Gold Medal**

**Women's
Professional
Soccer (WPS)
Goalkeeper of
the Year: 2009**

Played for
SAINT LOUIS
ATHLETICA
2009-10
Trophies:
*Regular Season
Champions*

**US Soccer
Female Athlete of
the Year: 2009**

**2011 FIFA
Women's World
Cup: Runner-up,
Golden Glove
& Bronze Ball**

A world-record crowd for a women's club match of 60,739 saw Atlético Madrid and Barcelona play in March 2019.

CHAMPION FOR CHANGE

Following the 2016 Olympic Games in Rio, the US took the controversial decision to terminate Hope's contract with the national team. In the aftermath of the United States quarter-final defeat to Sweden at the tournament, Hope had been critical of her opponents' overly defensive tactics, a remark that came from the heart rather than out of disrespect. Many of her teammates sided with the player, blaming the soccer federation for forcing Hope out of the team at a time when the keeper was campaigning for equal pay.

Today, Hope continues to dedicate her life to the game she loves and to making the world a better place for women everywhere. She is an advocate for the Women's Sports Foundation, a charity set up by legendary tennis player Billie Jean King to fight for equality in sport for every girl and woman, and is involved in girls' soccer programmes.

CASEY'S LOWDOWN

"Hope was an agile and confident goalkeeper. Her confidence and command of the box was incredible, and she never failed to deliver on the pitch."

Played for
ATLANTA
BEAT
2010
Teammates:
Eniola Aluko,
Tina Ellertson

Played for
MAGICJACK
2011

2012 London
Olympic Games:
Gold Medal

Played for
SEATTLE
SOUNDERS
WOMEN
2012
Teammates: Alex Morgan,
Megan Rapinoe

2015 FIFA Women's
World Cup: Winner
& Golden Glove

IFFHS World's
Best Woman
Goalkeeper:
2012, 2013,
2014, 2015

Played for
SEATTLE
REIGN
2013–16
Teammates:
Megan Rapinoe,
Amy Rodriguez

MARTA

MAGNIFICENT MARTA

Brilliant Brazilian Marta Vieira da Silva, known simply as Marta, is one of the finest players that women's football has ever produced. She has lit up stadiums with her magical skills and incredible goals, winning every individual prize in the game, as well as a host of trophies.

But her rise to the top was far from easy, Marta had to overcome prejudice and poverty, and to move far from home to achieve her dreams.

BREAKING BARRIERS

Marta grew up in Dois Riachos, located in Alagoas, one of the poorest states in Brazil. She was raised by her mother, along with three siblings, and often worked in the local market selling fruit and clothes to help her family. Her mother worked all day and had little time to spend with her children. There was no opportunity for a girl like Marta to go to school.

Marta began playing football when she was seven or eight years old in a country where football is a way of life. While crowds of boys were encouraged to kick deflated footballs, or ones fashioned from plastic shopping bags, around the streets, it was a different story for Marta, who was the only girl among them.

Between 1941 and 1979, Brazil's government banned women from playing football and other sports that were judged to be

'incompatible with their nature'. Even in the nineties, the stereotypes remained – a young Marta was regularly told she was 'not normal' for wanting to play in a boys' team, and 'not good enough', even though her skills easily outshone those of her teammates.

FORWARD

STATS

Country	Brazil
Club	Orlando Pride
Born	19 February 1986
Height	1.62 m
Club appearances	197
Club goals	139
International caps	147
International goals	112

Marta fought back by letting her feet do the talking. She joined a local junior boys' team. At the age of 14, she travelled for three days to the famous Brazilian club, Vasco da Gama, who were looking to establish a women's team. Her trial was successful and Marta moved more than 1,200 miles south of her hometown to Rio de Janeiro, where she spent two years playing for Vasco.

> # "My message to girls everywhere in this world: believe in yourself and trust yourself, because if you don't believe in yourself, no one else will."
>
> **MARTA**

Here are just some of the accolades that Marta has claimed over a 20-year career in women's football.

Played for
VASCO DA
GAMA
2000–02

Played for
SANTA
CRUZ
2002–04

**Pan
American
Games:
2003,
2007**

**Copa
América
Femenina:
2003,
2010,
2018**

Played for
UMEÅ IK
2004–08
Trophies:
*4 League Titles,
1 Swedish Cup,
1 UEFA Women's Cup*

SWEDISH SWITCH

As with many Brazilian players, both male and female, the best footballers work abroad for better opportunities and pay. At just 18 years old, Marta moved to Europe to join the Swedish club Umeå IK. She became the first Brazilian female to play the game professionally in Europe.

The transfer almost didn't go through – Umeå's manager spent months trying to get in contact with Marta, but she had no telephone in her house. Once she arrived, Marta was an instant hit, delighting fans by scoring an incredible 111 goals in just 103 appearances. Her goals were key to the club's success, helping them to win four league titles, the Swedish cup and the UEFA Women's Cup. In 2008, she left the club having been crowned FIFA Women's World Player of the Year for three years running to follow an American dream.

WINNING STREAK

Marta moved to America at a time where US women's football – or soccer – was booming. The newly formed Women's Professional Soccer (WPS) league was among the strongest in the world, with many of the world's top female players choosing to compete there. Spells with Los Angeles Sol, FC Gold Pride and Western New York Flash saw Marta twice win the WPS Championship, scoring a combined 40 goals in 60 appearances, while adding more goals back in Brazil for Santos in the off-seasons.

When the WPS folded in 2012, Marta returned to Sweden, this time with Tyresö FF on a big-money contract. The super striker helped the club to claim their first league title, while collecting her own fifth Swedish league winner's medal. Marta stayed at Tyresö for three seasons, moving to FC Rosengård in 2014, where she added to her

2004 Greece Olympic Games: Silver Medal

Top League Scorer 2004, 2005

The Best FIFA Women's Player: 2006, 2007, 2008, 2009, 2010, 2018

2007 FIFA Women's World Cup: Runners-up, Golden Ball & Golden Shoe

Top League Scorer 2008

2008 Beijing Olympic Games: Silver Medal

Played for
LOS ANGELES SOL
2009
Trophies: *Regular Season Champions*

honours. She returned to play in the US with Orlando Pride in 2017.

NATIONAL HERO

While Marta has won domestic trophies in both Europe and the United States, her performances for her own country have really earned her the reputation as a legend of the game. Brazil have come agonizingly close to becoming world and Olympic champions, thanks in no small part to Marta's dazzling displays for the Seleção, playing in an attacking trio with Cristiane and Formiga.

A 17-year-old Marta received her first call-up to the Brazil senior squad for the 2003 Women's World Cup in the United States. Her explosive performances and three goals helped Brazil to reach the quarter-finals. The following year, Marta scored three more goals at the Athens Olympics as the team took home the silver medal. They again

CASEY'S LOWDOWN

"An incredible player with a very special talent, Marta was one of the most creative forwards I had the privilege to play against. I had to be on the top of my game when I faced her at the London 2012 Olympics."

Top League Scorer: 2009, 2010, 2011

FIFA Women's World Cup Silver Shoe: 2011

Shortlisted for the Ballon d'Or Féminin: 2018

Played for
SANTOS
2009–10 (on loan)
Trophies:
*1 x Libertadores Cup,
1 x Brazilian Cup*

Played for
FC GOLD PRIDE
2010
Trophies:
*Play-off Champions,
Regular Season
Champions*

finished as runners-up at the 2007 World Cup in China, losing to Germany in the final. Marta's displays were magical – she picked up the Golden Ball for the tournament's best player and the Golden Shoe trophy for the top scorer with seven goals.

Marta cemented her place in Brazilian football history in 2008, when she left her footprints in the Walk of Fame outside Rio's famous Maracanã Stadium, alongside legends of the men's game, including Pelé and Ronaldinho.

Playing in her fourth World Cup in Canada in 2015, Marta became the tournament's record scorer, with 15 goals – one more strike than goal aces Birgit Prinz and Abby Wambach. Then, at the 2019 World Cup in France, Marta added two more strikes to become the all-time World Cup top scorer, male or female – an outstanding feat.

PROUD ROLE MODEL

Marta recognizes that sport changed her life completely. It gave her the opportunity to escape poverty, to help her family, to travel the world and to experience other cultures.

Thanks to Marta's work promoting women's football, there are now more opportunities for women to become professional footballers and to earn a living from playing the game they love. She hopes that her story and her work as a UN Women Goodwill Ambassador will inspire many more young girls and women to follow their dreams and discover their own talents.

One of the shining stars of the women's game, when Marta finally does hang up her boots, her glittering skills will never be forgotten.

Played for
WESTERN
NEW YORK FLASH
2011
Trophies:
*Play-off Champions,
Regular Season Champions*

Played for
TYRESÖ FF
2012–14
Trophies:
1 x League Title

Played for
FC ROSENGÅRD
2014–17
Trophies: *2 x League
Titles*
Teammates:
Lieke Martens

Played for
ORLANDO
PRIDE
2017–present
Teammates:
*Alex Morgan,
Sydney Leroux*

CHRISTINE SINCLAIR

STRIKING OUT

Strong striker Christine is the most successful player in Canada's history. Head and shoulders above the competition, she has been named the country's female player of the year no fewer than 14 times during a brilliant career in football.

From scoring her debut goal for Canada as a 16-year-old, Christine has racked up a phenomenal 182 goals for her country, just two strikes short of the world record set by the USA's Abby Wambach, who scored 184 international goals. If Christine goes on to claim this honour while playing for a Canadian team that has risen from an average position to become a top-five international side, it would be a remarkable achievement that may never be beaten.

HIGH SCHOOL HERO

Born and raised in Burnaby, Canada, Christine began playing football at the tender age of four. Anything her big brother could do, Christine was determined to do better, so she joined an under-sevens team, playing against kids who were much stronger and bigger than she was.

While at high school, she led her side to three league championships and caught the eye of Canada's national team coach. She made her senior international debut as a 16-year-old at the 2000 Algarve Cup, where she also scored her first international goal. Even then, Christine was playing with a

SINCLAIR 12

FORWARD/ MIDFIELDER

STATS

Country .... Canada

Club .... Portland Thorns FC

Born .... 12 June 1983

Height .... 1.75 m

Club appearances 197

Club goals 87

International caps 286

International goals 182

maturity beyond her years – reading the game well, picking out passes and looking dangerous whenever the ball was at her feet.

Christine went on to study at the prestigious University of Portland in the United States, where she played soccer for the college side. By the time she graduated in 2005, she was the all-time leading scorer in the history of the university's women's soccer programme. Christine continued to play for the national under-19s and senior sides at Portland, and signed for FC Gold Pride, based in Santa Clara, California, once her studies were complete.

WORLD STAGE

Christine headed to her first World Cup in 2003 at the age of 20. Her three goals for Canada helped to take the team to their best finish yet – an unexpected fourth place. Having never won a match at any previous World Cup, Canada's performance marked a historic improvement for the team, although Team Canada have not reached the knock-out stages at a World Cup since.

Christine has competed in three Olympic Games: Beijing 2008, London 2012 and at Rio 2016, claiming a bronze medal in both London and Rio. She captained the team in London and was the tournament's leading scorer. She scored six of Canada's 12 goals, including a hat-trick in their controversial semi-final extra-time defeat of the United States. Their bronze-medal win was Canada's first medal in a traditional

Canadian Player of the Year: **2000, 2004–14, 2016, 2018**

Played for
VANCOUVER BREAKERS
2001–02

Played for
VANCOUVER WHITECAPS FC
2006–08

team sport at the summer games since 1936. Christine was given the honour of being Canada's flag-bearer for the closing ceremony at the Games in recognition of her efforts. Team Canada again took the bronze medal in Rio, this time beating Marta's Brazil with a winning goal from Sinclair to claim a famous third-place finish. Among Christine's next goals is competing at a fourth Games in Tokyo and winning a third Olympic medal.

CLUB SUCCESS

Christine has played club football in the United States' top tier with three different clubs. Her first campaign as a senior was with FC Gold Pride in the first season of the Women's Professional Soccer league (WPS). A strong side that saw Christine play alongside Marta, France's Camille Abily and the USA's Shannon Boxx dominated the league, winning the WPS Championship. The club disbanded at the end of the 2009–10 season for financial reasons.

The world-class attacker moved to Western New York Flash in 2011, where she guided the team to the championship with 10 goals and eight assists, earning herself the title of the team's 'Most Valuable Player' (MVP). The league was suspended in 2012 and the National Women's Soccer League (NWSL) replaced it.

Christine switched sides to join the Portland Thorns in 2013, a club that boasted USA internationals Alex Morgan and Tobin Heath on its roster. She has captained the side to two championships during her time there. While critics note that Christine never signed with a top European club, what cannot be questioned is her commitment and outstanding contribution to every team in which she has played.

Played for
FC GOLD PRIDE
2009–10
Trophies: *1 x US League Title*
Teammates: *Marta*

Played for
WESTERN NEW YORK FLASH
2011–12
Trophies: *1 x US League Title*
Teammates:
Alex Morgan, Marta

2012 London Olympic Games: Bronze Medal & Leading Scorer

"One of the strongest forwards I faced, Christine caused me the greatest heartache with her goals for Canada against Team GB in the London 2012 Olympics quarter-final."

ROLE MODEL

Naturally shy and humble, Christine has never been comfortable with the label 'best player in the world', despite her multiple nominations for the FIFA Women's World Player of the Year award. A player that has shone throughout the decades as the women's game has developed, Christine realized that sharing her story could be an inspiration to others.

The forward has made a career playing sport in an exciting time for women, where goals that were once thought to be unachievable are now possible. Christine is a firm believer that barriers are made to be broken, and will continue to coach younger players to believe that they can do anything if they work hard and follow their passion.

Played for
PORTLAND THORNS
2013–present
Trophies: *2 x US League Titles*
Teammates:
Alex Morgan, Nadine Angerer

2016 Rio Olympic Games: Bronze Medal

Awarded the Order of Canada in 2017

Shortlisted for the Ballon d'Or Féminin: 2018

"If they think your dreams are crazy, show them what crazy dreams can do."

CHRISTINE SINCLAIR

LUCY BRONZE

SOLID BRONZE

Lucia Roberta Tough Bronze is better known as 'Lucy' Bronze, the brilliant right-back who has featured in the world's top 10 female players for several seasons.

Her calm and solid performances for England and for European Champions Lyon have taken her game to the very top, leading the Lionesses' boss, Phil Neville, to claim that Lucy could easily play in the men's game. In 2018, Lucy was shortlisted for the first Ballon d'Or award, to celebrate the best player in women's football.

GIRL POWER

Born in Berwick-upon-Tweed in the northeast of England, Lucy played for local youth side Alnwick Town growing up. One of her early memories in football was as a 10-year-old in a match when an opponent complained it would be 'too easy playing against a girl', while others laughed from the sidelines. It would not be the first time that Lucy would have the last laugh by outclassing a boy.

While on the pitch, Lucy could overcome any challenge that faced her, but it wasn't so easy to prove herself off the pitch. She was forced to quit the under-12s team, as FA rules banned mixed teams for older age groups. At the time, Lucy was devastated. The ban meant that she was split up from her childhood teammates, her friends, and she faced a long drive to train in Blyth and

later Sunderland. Lucy's family helped to campaign for a change in the rules, and the age limit for mixed teams was raised to 16 in 2014 and then to 18 in 2015. Now, in the UK, girls have the choice to play against boys or for girls-only teams.

GOING PRO

Bronze began her professional career with Sunderland, winning the player-of-the-match award in the FA Cup Final in 2009 when she was just 17 years old, despite the Black Cats losing to Arsenal. That summer, Lucy went to study at the University of North Carolina in the United States. She had won a scholarship and played for the

DEFENDER

BRONZE

2

STATS

Country .... England

Club .... Olympique Lyonnais

Born .... 28 October 1991

Height .... 1.72 m

Club appearances 164

Club goals 21

International caps 75

International goals 8

Just 1% of all sports advertising revenue is allocated to women's sport, even less to women's football.

college side's football team, the Tar Heels. Lucy returned to Sunderland in 2010 before a move to Everton, where she featured in the UEFA Women's Champions League for the first time. A switch to rivals Liverpool followed, where Lucy's classy defensive displays helped the team to win back-to-back league titles in 2013 and 2014.

A move to the newly formed Manchester City then followed, and the team went undefeated for the entire season in 2016 with Lucy forming part of a mean defence. The Sky Blues qualified for the Champions League for the first time in Lucy's debut season at the club.

NEW ADVENTURE

Three major trophies later, Lucy was ready for a fresh challenge. She earned a contract with European giants Lyon, who announced they had signed 'the best full-back in the world'. Lucy slotted straight in to the star-studded side with captain Wendie Renard, Ada Hegerberg and Dzsenifer Marozsán, as she kicked on to raise her game a level. Lucy's number-one goal of winning the UEFA Champion's League was achieved in her first campaign with Lyon, as the defender scored a sensational volley – a goal that was nominated for UEFA's goal-of-the-year award – to knock out former club Manchester City in the semi-finals. Lucy admits she loves chipping in with a goal to help her team whenever she can, and has scored at each of her clubs throughout her career.

PLAYING FOR ENGLAND

Lucy first represented her country for England's under-17 side while playing for the girls' side, Blyth Town. Things might have been very different had Lucy accepted an invitation to play for Portugal at around the age of 16, which she was eligible for through her Portuguese father. She has no regrets that she chose the Lionesses: England are performing among the very best teams in the world.

At the age of 18, Lucy suffered the first of four knee injuries during a period that would prove to be the toughest time in her career. Lucy was out injured for a whole year and didn't complete a full 90 minutes for nearly two years. She received no help to get back on her feet from the FA, which didn't have the funds to rehabilitate young players. She was told she might never play for England again, and even now, she never takes her place for granted. Through hard work and self-belief, Lucy overcame her injury and returned to England, winning her first senior cap at the age of 23.

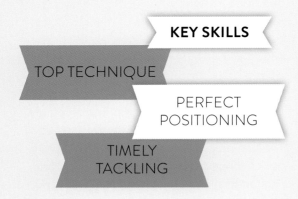

KEY SKILLS

TOP TECHNIQUE

PERFECT POSITIONING

TIMELY TACKLING

"As female athletes, we need to be able to express ourselves. Sometimes, that's through talking and telling your story. But I want to target the boys as well, because ultimately it's society [...] that you try to change. It's important [that] women are empowered to do anything."

LUCY BRONZE

In 2015, Lucy was selected in the World Cup squad to go to Canada, a tournament in which she shone as a big-match performer. The full-back scored the winning goal from outside the box as England came from behind to beat Norway 2–1 in the round of the last 16. Then in the quarter-finals, Lucy netted a winning header to beat the hosts, Canada. England claimed third place – their best finish – and returned home to find that many people's perceptions of women's football had changed.

In 2018, Lucy captained the Lionesses for the first time at the SheBelieves cup, a tournament that England would go on to win in 2019. It was a stellar year for the defender, as she became the first English player to receive the BBC Women's Footballer of the Year, an award voted for by fans from across the world. Lucy was surprised to win, but proud to fly the flag for defenders, who are often overlooked in favour of goalscorers.

A string of fine performances and another wonder goal at the World Cup in France in 2019 saw Lucy take home the Silver Ball, an award for the tournament's second-best player. Lucy has proved that not only is she a leading Lioness, but she can comfortably compete among the best players in the world. Having worked incredibly hard to build herself back up from from injury, the award is all the sweeter – Lucy is an inspiration to young footballers everywhere.

CASEY'S LOWDOWN

"An incredible athlete with a fantastic will to win. Lucy was once told by her coaches that she would never make it... she's now the best attacking right-back in the world."

Played for
SUNDERLAND
2007–10
Trophies: *1 x FA Women's Premier League Northern Division*

Played for
EVERTON
2010–12
Teammates: *Toni Duggan*

Played for
LIVERPOOL
2012–14
Trophies: *2 x League Titles*
Teammates: *Fara Williams*

MANCHESTER CITY
2014–17
Trophies: *1 x League Title, 1 x English Cup, 1 x WSL Cup*
Teammates: *Karen Bardsley, Nikita Parris, Steph Houghton*

PFA Women's Player of the Year 2014, 2017

OLYMPIQUE LYONNAIS
2017–present
Trophies: *2 x French League Titles,*
1 x UEFA Champions League Title,
1 x French Cup
Teammates: *Wendie Renard,*
Ada Hegerberg,
Dzsenifer Marozsán

***Shortlisted
for the
Ballon d'Or
Féminin:
2018***

***2018 BBC Women's
Footballer of
the Year: Winner***

***FIFA Women's World
Cup Silver Ball: 2019***

PERNILLE HARDER

GREAT DANE

Fantastic forward Pernille Harder is playing the best football of her career, leading the line for her club and country. Pernille loves to beat players, has excellent technique and a sharp eye for goal, leading many to claim that the dazzling Dane is the most complete women's footballer in the world.

A striker who always dreamed of making it the top, success in the Champions League with her German club Wolfsburg, and on the world stage with Denmark, are Pernille's next targets.

CLEAR FOCUS

Pernille first began playing football aged five or six and she competed against boys until she was 11. Girls' teams in the small town of Ikast in the heart of Denmark simply did not exist. Even though she was the only girl in the team, the boys definitely wanted the clever goalscorer on their side, and Pernille felt accepted.

It may have been destiny that Pernille became a footballer, and it certainly helped that both her parents and her elder sister played the game too. Pernille wanted to do everything that her sister Louise did. At school, around the age of 10, Pernille wrote that she wanted to play professional club football in Germany and represent Denmark internationally. At a time when the professional game was in its infancy, it took her just 15 years for her to realize both dreams.

Pernille's senior career began with local club Team Viborg at the age of 15, and she was called up to the national side to face Georgia when she was just 16. Her debut was a special one – the teenager scored a hat-trick in a devastating 15–0 victory.

She began making a name for herself at home, scoring 22 goals in 27 games for IK Skovbakken in Denmark's top division, the Elitedivisionen, before a bigger team came calling. Pernille moved to Swedish side Linköping aged 19, at a time when Tyresö FF and Rosengård were dominating Sweden's top women's league. Harder's contribution was clear – by 2016 she was one of the top strikers in the division. Linköping won the Damallsvenskan League title, finishing 10

FORWARD

STATS

Country .... Denmark
Club .... VfL Wolfsburg
Born .... 15 November 1992
Height .... 1.68 m
Club appearances 167
Club goals 132
International caps 105
International goals 53

points ahead of second-placed Rosengård. Pernille was part of a dynamic young team that was going places. She was now a league winner with 50 caps for her country, and top clubs from all over Europe enquired after the striker's services.

DREAM MOVE

Pernille had been desperate to play in Germany, and she joined German club Wolfsburg for the second half of the 2016–17 Bundesliga campaign. This was one of the best clubs in Europe and the striker was keen to stretch herself. She felt that she had learned all she could from Swedish football. But the decision wasn't easy –

Harder had to leave behind her girlfriend, teammate Magda Eriksson, who herself later moved to Chelsea.

Wolfsburg has been a happy hunting ground for Pernille – she has twice won the German League and the cup, playing in a strong side that has included Nilla Fischer, Alexandra Popp and goalkeeper Almuth Schult. German football is traditionally physical and more attacking, which suits Pernille's fast, attacking style of play.

Wolfsburg missed out on the treble in 2017–18 when they lost to Lyon in the final of the UEFA Women's Champions League. Pernille had put her team ahead with a strike

"I always dreamed of being one of the biggest players in women's football and of being able to change things."

PERNILLE HARDER

during extra time in Kiev, but Lyon battled back to win 4–1. The following season, Wolfsburg were again knocked out of the competition by rivals Lyon, with Pernille leading the goal-scoring charts with eight goals. With her best years still ahead of her, expect more trophies yet.

INTERNATIONAL DUTY

Pernille has played international football for Denmark for a decade, winning over a century of caps and scoring more than 50 goals, including six hat-tricks. A leader on and off the pitch, Pernille was made captain of the Danish Dynamite in March 2016. The highlight of her time on international duty was when Denmark reached the final of the UEFA Women's Championship in 2017, which was held in the Netherlands. It was a Danish performance that surprised many, with the side tipped as outsiders for the tournament. Having lost to the Netherlands in the group stage, the teams met again at the final. Harder scored a superb solo first-half goal – her only strike of the competition – to level the scores, but the hosts were too strong and went on to win 4–2. Despite the loss, interest in women's football spiked in Denmark following the tournament, earning the players a new respect among fans.

The heartbreak continued in 2019 when Denmark again lost to the Netherlands in the European play-off semi-finals during World Cup qualification. Ada Hegerberg was taking a break from the Norway team due to frustrations with the Norwegian FA at a lack of support for women's football, so the tournament in France was played without two of the game's most talented players.

Denmark's bid to stage the Women's European Championship in 2025 may allow Pernille her time to shine on home soil, by which time the forward will be 32.

Played for
TEAM
VIBORG
2007–10

Played for
IK
SKOVBAKKEN
2010–12

Played for
LINKÖPINGS FC
2012–16
Trophies:
1 x Swedish League Titles,
2 x Swedish Cups,
2 x Swedish Super Cups

Danish Footballer
Player of the Year:
2015, 2016

2017
UEFA Women's
Championship:
Runner-up

MODEL PROFESSIONAL

Pernille's skilled performances and reputation have earned her the status of role model for girls growing up not just in Denmark, but all over the world. The striker is proud that women footballers can now be idols for both girls and boys. Her own role model growing up was Brazil's record goalscorer, Marta, who has won a host of individual awards and is still a force in the women's game.

Pernille's first major prize was UEFA's Player of the Year award for 2017–18, where the striker beat a strong field, including Norway's Ada Hegerberg and France's Amandine Henry. It was the first time that a Danish player had claimed the award and a proud moment for Pernille, who sees the prize as a motivation to keep working hard to achieve all she can.

KEY SKILLS

TOP TECHNIQUE

TIMELY TACKLING

PERFECT POSITIONING

CASEY'S LOWDOWN

"A highly intelligent player, Pernille knows how to find the space to create chances that other players don't see. She has great technical ability and would boss any midfield."

UEFA Women's Player of the Year: 2017–18

Bundesliga top scorer: 2017–18

Played for
VFL WOLFSBURG
2017–present
Trophies: 3 x German League Titles, 3 x German Cups
Teammates: Caroline Graham Hansen, Alexandra Popp, Mary Earps

Shortlisted for the Ballon d'Or Féminin: 2018

2019 BBC Women's Footballer of the Year: Winner

ALEX MORGAN

AMERICAN HERO

Californian Alex Morgan has been one of the most important players in the United States squad since 2011, when she became the youngest player in a World Cup Squad at the 2011 tournament in Germany.

While injury delayed her debut for the national side – Alex was 20 years old when she won her first cap against Mexico – the forward has since played more than 160 times for her country, scoring a century of goals. Her quality in front of goal and her ability to score on the biggest of stages have proved priceless, contributing to an Olympic Gold Medal at London 2012 and World Cup glory in 2015.

Alex is the youngest of three co-captains for the United States, alongside teammates Carli Lloyd and Megan Rapinoe. Her club career has seen Alex win the national championship with two different clubs, while a half-season loan to Lyon earned her three more major trophies.

DIAMOND GIRL

Alex was born in Diamond City, California, in the United States. From the age of five, she could be found kicking a ball around her back garden, or racing her two older sisters down the street. Growing up, Alex excelled in a number of sports, including sprinting, but didn't join a formal football club until her early teens. Her dad loved baseball and knew nothing about soccer, but signed up

to become a referee and then a coach when his daughter caught the football bug. By the age of 13, Alex had become one of the best recreational players in Southern California, all while wearing hand-me-down boots. That same year, her dad took Alex shopping and bought her the most expensive boots in the shop. The investment paid off, as Alex would later go on to become a world and Olympic champion with the United States.

While she was at high school Alex was fast-tracked to the national Olympic Development Program, which allowed her to train with the best coaches and against the best players. At 17, the forward was

FORWARD

STATS

Country: ....United States

Club: ....Portland Thorns

Born: .... 2 July 1989

Height: ....1.70 m

Club caps: 116

Club goals: 52

International caps: 169

International goals: 107

called up to the United States under-20 squad, but she suffered her first devastating injury while playing in a friendly match. It was a tough time for Alex and she was sidelined for months. Just as they had been there for her at every practice and every match, it was her mum and dad who helped Alex to get back on her feet.

Alex returned to the game stronger, playing for the University of California, Berkeley's side, the California Golden Bears, alongside the under-20s. Her first senior call-up came in March 2010 during the forward's final semester at Berkeley.

GAME-CHANGER

A month later, Alex announced herself on the world stage. The World Cup was set to take place the following summer in Germany. As two-time World Champions,

the United States side had never failed to qualify for the tournament. But, defeat to Mexico during qualification meant that they faced a play-off against Italy. The winner would take the remaining place at the World Cup finals – defeat was unthinkable. The first leg was played in Italy, and remained deadlocked as the final whistle approached. Alex came on as a substitute with just four minutes to go and scored with an angled shot from the edge of the box, deep into injury time. It was the biggest goal in her short career, and was the start of what would be a pattern of her scoring crucial late goals.

At 21 years old, Alex was the youngest player in the United States World Cup squad the following summer. In the semi-final against France, the forward popped up again at the 82nd minute to secure a 3–1 win. In the World Cup final,

the United States faced Japan. Alex entered the play as a half-time substitute with the scores at 0–0. It took her less than 15 minutes to put the United States ahead, and she later provided an assist for Abby Wambach during extra time. The US were defeated in a penalty shoot-out, but Morgan had shown her mettle.

The year 2012 saw the Olympics held in London. It was a special year for Alex. Her heroics in London – two goals and three assists in the first stages of the tournament – saw the United States progress to the semi-finals. In a thrilling affair, a hat-trick from Canada's Christine Sinclair looked likely to send the USA home – until a Wambach penalty levelled the scores. This time, Alex left it nail-bitingly late to score a winning header in the 123rd minute, causing heartbreak for Canada and elation for the USA.

CASEY'S LOWDOWN

"I faced Alex when she was breaking into the United States squad in 2011. Pacy and creative, it was clear that she had a bright future in the game."

In the gold-medal match, the US lined up against world champions Japan. Revenge was sweet as the United States took the gold in front of more than 80,000 spectators at London's Wembley Stadium – a record crowd!

In 2015, Alex became a world champion at last – at the 2015 world cup in Canada.

Played for
WEST
COAST FC
2008–09

Played for
CALIFORNIA
STORM
2010

Played for
PALI
BLUES
2010

Played for
WESTERN
NEW YORK
FLASH
2011
Trophies:
1 x US League Title

Played for
SEATTLE
SOUNDERS
2012

In several countries, it is actually illegal for women and girls to play football – including in Saudi Arabia and Iran.

The forward played in all seven of the USA's matches, including the team's 5–2 victory over Japan to win the trophy. Alex and her teammates became the first women's sports team to be honoured with a ticker-tape parade through New York City following their success at the tournament. By 2019, the United States' golden girl had scored 100 goals for her country. Alex's goal-scoring form continued at the 2019 World Cup, as the forward scored for the Champions six times – including a record five goals in one match against Thailand to claim the Silver Shoe trophy.

CLUB FOOTBALL

Alex has enjoyed success playing in the United States' top league, winning the WPS title with Western New York Flash and the NWSL Championship with the Portland Thorns. Aged 27, while in the prime of her career, Alex took a risk and accepted a loan move to Lyon, a club that is committed to providing equal opportunities for male and female players. Her dream to test herself against the best players in the world paid off, and Alex returned to Portland with Champions League, French Championship and French Cup winners' medals.

OFF THE PITCH

Alex has always been brave enough to stand up for what she believes is right. In 2016, she and US teammates Megan Rapinoe, Hope Solo and Carli Lloyd filed a wage-discrimination action against the US Soccer Federation. That year, the Federation paid its female stars just a quarter of the men's team's salary, despite the women's side becoming World Champions the previous year, and generating millions more in profit. The lawsuit is ongoing.

2012 London Olympic Games: Gold Medal

FIFA World Player of the Year: finalist: 2012

Played for
PORTLAND THORNS FC
2013–15
Trophies:
1 x US League Title

2011 FIFA Women's World Cup: Runner-up

US Soccer Athlete of the Year: 2012, 2018

2015 FIFA Women's World Cup: Winner

Since 2015, Alex has been the top-earning women's player in the world, thanks to a number of lucrative endorsements with sports brands and advertisers. She was one of the first players to sign up to the 'Common Goal' campaign, an initiative that sees both male and female players donate 1 percent of their salaries to help inspire disadvantaged young people through football projects.

Alex is also the author of a successful series of football-themed children's books, *The Kicks*, which was adapted for TV in the US. She hopes to continue her work with UNICEF as a Global Athlete Ambassador when she calls time on her playing career.

> "Always work hard, never give up, and fight until the end because it's never really over until the final whistle blows."
>
> **ALEX MORGAN**

KEY SKILLS

GLORIOUS GOALS RECORD

INCREDIBLE SPEED

SPECTACULAR SHOTS

Played for
OLYMPIQUE LYONNAIS
2017 (on loan)
Trophies: *1 x French League Title, 1 x French Cup, 1 x Champions League Title*
Teammates: *Wendie Renard, Ada Hegerberg, Saki Kumagai*

Played for
ORLANDO PRIDE
2016–present
Teammates:
Ashlyn Harris, Marta

2019 FIFA Women's World Cup: Winner & Silver Shoe Winner

SAM KERR

SHARP SHOOTER

Unstoppable striker Sam grew up playing Aussie rules football, a game played with an oval-shaped ball. As she got older, the game became rougher, and Sam made the switch to soccer at the age of 12.

Incredibly, just three years later, she was playing football for the Australian national women's team, the Matildas. Since then Sam has taken the game by storm, smashing goal records in Australia's W-League and the top league in the USA, the NWSL, becoming one of the hardest-working players in football. Still only in her mid-twenties, the fearless young striker has warned opponents there's more to come.

FORWARD

STATS

Country: .... Australia
Club: .... Chicago Red Stars
Born: .... 10 September 1993
Height: .... 1.67 m
Club caps: 193
Club goals: 126
International caps: 81
International goals: 36

AUSSIE GIRL

Sam was born in Fremantle, a suburb of Perth, Western Australia, to an Anglo-Indian father and an Australian mother. At home, Australian rules football ruled, as both her father and brother played the sport professionally. Sam at first followed in their footsteps, but there was no route for girls to play at a professional level at the time.

She discovered football aged 12, fell in love with the game after a year, and could usually be found playing against boys while wearing a David Beckham or Cristiano Ronaldo shirt. By 15, Sam was developing her game at a remarkable pace. She earned her first senior call-up to the Australian national side in a match against Italy. Her first goal came

when Sam opened the scoring in the 2010 Asian Cup final against North Korea, which Australia went on to win 5–4 on penalties. She was only 16.

The striker has since starred on the international stage for a whole decade, helping the Matildas to win the Asian Cup in 2009, as well as the Tournament of Nations, a four-team competition in which Sam was the leading scorer in 2017. The goal ace can also list three World Cups and an Olympic Games in which she has represented Australia – an incredible career for such a young player. She was rewarded for her efforts with the national team by being promoted to team captain in February

"It's tough, but I love what I do, so I'm lucky and I don't take it for granted. There would be a million people wishing they could do what I'm doing."

SAM KERR

2019, aged 25. Sam's dream is to one day win a major tournament, and she would happily swap her individual awards to lead the Matildas to glory. Until then, she will carry on playing the game she loves and bringing out her famous trademark goal celebration – a self-taught backflip that thrills the crowds.

SUPERSTAR STATUS

In the domestic game, Sam made her debut for Perth Glory while she was still a schoolgirl. She remains the youngest debutant in the W-League (15 years and 45 days) as well as its youngest goalscorer (15 years and 88 days). Her first trophy was won with Sydney FC, the W-League Championship in 2012–13.

Since 2013, Sam has juggled playing commitments in two different continents, dominating Australia's W-League from October to February and the United States' NWSL from April to October. The striker rarely wastes an opportunity to score – Sam can shoot with her left foot, her right foot and can use her incredible leap to score headed goals, too. She has overcome three serious injuries to earn the record for the most goals scored in a season in both leagues, with Perth Glory and former club Sky Blue FC, and has become one of the most-wanted players in the world.

Sam was transferred to the NSWL club the Chicago Red Stars in January 2018. In October that year, the Football Federation of Australia unveiled Sam as the W-League's first female marquee signing when she re-signed for Perth. They agreed to pay the striker substantially more than the league's salary cap. The FFA recognized Sam's contribution to promoting the women's game, and it was an important step towards achieving equal pay for women in sport.

Played for
PERTH GLORY
*2008–11,
2014–19*
Trophies:
*1 x Australian
League Title*

**2010
AFC
*Women's
Asian Cup:*
Winner**

Played for
SYDNEY FC
2012–14
Trophies:
1 x Australian League
Teammate:
Caitlin Foord

Played for
WESTERN
NEW YORK FLASH
2013–14
Trophies: *1 x NWSL Shield*
Teammates:
Carli Lloyd, Abbi Wambach

FAN CLUB

Sam is a role model for all. Her special talent and exciting play attract fans of all ages and genders. Just hours after the 2019 World Cup Matildas kit was released, the men's cut – many of which were customized with 'KERR' on the back – had sold out. Sam didn't disappoint at the World Cup, scoring five goals in four matches at the tournament.

So what's next for the hungry striker? While Sam has admitted that she'd love to win more trophies with Perth Glory, a switch to European football could be in store, as she looks to take her game to the next level. She has twice been nominated for the FIFA Best Women's Player award, and she made the Ballon d'Or longlist in 2018.

A successful transfer to one of Europe's top leagues would make it seriously hard for selectors not to consider finally crowning Sam as the world's best player. Chelsea and Barcelona are just two clubs that have reportedly shown an interest in signing the Australian skipper. Wherever her next move may take her, one thing is guaranteed: Sam will be a special player, a leader, but first and foremost will play with a smile on her face.

CASEY'S LOWDOWN

"Frighteningly fast, Sam is a clinical forward who can create space for herself to finish from any area."

Played for
SKY BLUE
FC
2015–17
Teammate:
Caitlin Foord

**2010 AFC
Women's
Asian Cup:
Winner**

**Asian Women's
Footballer
of the Year:
2017**

Played for
CHICAGO
RED STARS
2017–present
Teammates:
*Julie Ertz,
Casey Short*

**NWSL
Most Valuable
Player: 2017**

**2017
Tournament
of Nations:
Winner**

KEY SKILLS

GLORIOUS
GOALS RECORD

TOP
TECHNIQUE

SUPER GOAL
CELEBRATION

*NWSL
Golden Boot:
2017, 2018*

*All-time record
for goals scored
in the NWSL*

*Shortlisted
for the
BBC Women's
Footballer
of the Year
2019*

*Shortlisted for
the Ballon d'Or
Féminin:
2018*

*All-time record
for goals scored
in the W-League*

SAKI KUMAGAI

CLASS OF HER OWN

Calm and classy midfielder Saki Kumagai is Japan's captain and one of Asia's greatest sporting exports. While she plays in central defence for Japan, Saki enjoys a more advanced role in the heart of her club Lyon's midfield.

While playing the role of a defensive midfielder, linking defence with attack, Saki hasn't always been given the credit she deserves. But look at her honours for club and country, and her contribution to her teams is clear. Kumagai is a world champion with Japan and a European champion with Lyon, playing a neat, assured style of football that has seen her develop into one of the very best players in women's football.

KUMAGAI 4

DEFENDER/ MIDFIELDER

STATS

Country: ....Japan

Club: .... Olympique Lyonnais

Born: ....17 October 1990

Height: ....1.73 m

Club caps: 238

Club goals: 34

International caps: 108

International goals: 0

STARTING OUT

Saki was born in Sapporo, Japan, in 1990. Growing up, the first club she played for was a boys' club. Makomanai-Minami Soccer Sport Boys' Club allowed girls and boys to train together as no girls' clubs existed at the time. She showed off her skills playing for Tokiwaki Gakuen High School, and signed for the top-flight Urawa Red Diamonds in 2009, a club based near Tokyo, after graduating. The Diamonds won the championship in Saki's first season there, but women's football in Japan was poorly paid with small attendances at games. While the J-League attracted investment to develop the men's game, women's football was largely ignored.

In 2008 aged 17, she made her debut for the national side against Canada, and captained the under-20s team two years later at the 2010 U-20 World Cup.

Then, in the summer of 2011, Saki's life was to change forever. The Japan international moved to Europe to play with German Bundesliga club FFC Frankfurt, and she was selected for Japan's World Cup squad.

WORLD CUP WINNER

Japan qualified for the 2011 World Cup in Germany, having finished third in the Asian Cup. They had failed to advance from the group stages at the previous tournaments, and were not even considered as outsiders – let alone contenders – for the title. Placed in a group with England, Mexico and New Zealand, Japan finished second to set up a quarter-final against the hosts in Wolfsburg. A single goal sealed victory after extra time for Japan, as the Nadeshiko progressed to the semi-finals against Sweden. Japan came from behind to run out 3–1 winners. They then faced the tournament favourites, the United States, in the final. The match was played in Frankfurt, the city where Saki had just signed to play club football.

Japan had shown a great team spirit throughout the tournament, playing with composure under pressure, and the final was no different. The United States twice went in front, but a late equalizer from legend Homare Sawa meant that the match would be decided by a penalty shoot-out. Saki was just 20 years old when she coolly slotted home the winning penalty against the world's number-one keeper, Hope Solo.

The World Cup was awarded to the unfancied Japan, a nation still reeling from a devastating earthquake and tsunami that had hit the country a few months earlier. Saki and her teammates became overnight sensations in Japan, as the team overtook China as the best side in Asia. Finally, women's football in Japan would start to be taken seriously.

GROWING REPUTATION

The following year, Japan went to the London 2012 Olympics with Saki now a key player in the squad. The team were keen to show that their World Cup win was not a one-off. They reached the final unbeaten. Japan again faced the United States in the gold-medal decider, but this time were

Played for
URAWA
RED DIAMONDS
2009–11

2010 Asian Games: Gold Medal

2011 FIFA Women's World Cup: Winner

Played for
FFC
FRANKFURT
2011–13

2012 London Olympic Games: Silver Medal

Played for
OLYMPIQUE LYONNAIS
2013–present
Trophies: *6 x League Titles, 5 x French Cups,*
4 x UEFA Champions League Titles
Teammates: *Amadine Henry,*
Ada Hegerberg, Wendie Renard

2015 FIFA
Women's World
Cup: Runner-up

2018 AFC
Women's Asian
Cup: Winner

Shortlisted for
the Ballon d'Or
Féminin 2018

Shortlisted for
the BBC Women's
Footballer of the
Year 2019

"It doesn't matter to me whether a player is young or a veteran. The one thing I do tell anyone is to be aggressive – to go all in."

SAKI KUMAGAI

CASEY'S LOWDOWN

"The Rolls-Royce of the Japanese midfield, Saki is strong with both feet and has an unbelievable range of passing. She seems to have all the time in the world on the ball."

narrowly defeated 2–1 at Wembley Stadium in front of more than 80,000 fans. A silver medal belonged to Saki.

The Nadeshiko headed to the 2015 World Cup in Canada hoping to retain the crown they had won in Germany, and again reached the final, thanks to the team's confident and calm displays. In a rematch of the 2011 final, this time old foes the United States were unstoppable, racing into a 4–0 lead after just 16 minutes. The match ended 5–2, a score that Japan fans hope will never be repeated.

LEADING BY EXAMPLE

Since 2013, Saki has played her club football in France with European champions, Lyon. A key cog in Lyon's world-class midfield, Saki has won five French League titles, four French cups and an incredible

treble of Champions League trophies. A highlight of her time with Lyon was the 2016 Champions League final. In a tense affair, an Ada Hegerberg goal gave Lyon an early lead, but Wolfsburg's Alexandra Popp levelled the scores with just two minutes to go. Extra time was played, followed by a penalty shoot-out. Saki used the memory of her World Cup-winning penalty to convert the final spot-kick for Lyon, clinching a 4–3 victory. Saki lifted the European trophy having been named the player of the match.

Kumagai, a perfect mentor for younger players, has been captain of Japan since 2017. She has earned a century of caps for her country. In 2020, Saki and Japan will carry the hopes of a nation on their shoulders at the Tokyo Olympics. Winning a second Olympic medal, this time on home soil, may yet top Saki's list of highlights in a stunning career in football.

LIEKE MARTENS

LIVING A DREAM

Netherlands hero Lieke grew up in Bergen, a tiny village of just a few thousand people, next to the border with Germany.

Her earliest memory of football is of kicking a small ball around on the sidelines while she watched her older brothers play in matches. Once she was five years old she could join in herself. While her friends played with Barbie dolls after school, Lieke would join her brothers and their friends in games of football. She became known in the village as the little girl who was never without her beloved ball, spending hours practising her technique against a wall. At her first club,

Lieke was happy that the boys accepted her on their team, no doubt because of her skills. Opponents were much less friendly, but Lieke stayed strong. She played with and against boys until she was 16, and believes this made her a more competitive player.

Now a free-scoring forward for Barcelona and the Netherlands national team, Lieke is living her dream, having fun 'every single day' as one of the top women footballers.

MAKING SACRIFICES

When Lieke was 15, everything changed. She was invited to the under-19 squad for the national side. Since they were based in the Dutch capital, Amsterdam, Lieke had to move away from home and leave her family and friends behind. The teenager had to teach herself how to cook and do her own laundry, which often ended in shrunken clothes and kitchen disasters. She often felt lonely in a team of older girls of 18 or 19 years old, and had to grow up quickly. She missed her family, her two brothers and her little sister, who was only eight when Lieke left home. But Lieke dreamed of becoming a professional footballer and understood that sacrifices would have to be made if she was to make it to the top.

In 2011, she made her debut for the Netherlands senior side aged 18, and moved to the top Belgian team, Standard Liège, winning her first trophy with the club. Lieke was selected for the Netherlands Euro 2013 squad, but the team finished a disappointing

MARTENS 11

FORWARD

STATS

Country .... Netherlands

Club .... FC Barcelona Femení

Born .... 16 December 1992

Height .... 1.70 m

Club appearances 208

Club goals 87

International caps 110

International goals 44

More than 750 million television viewers around the world watched the FIFA Women's World Cup Canada 2015.

··

CASEY'S LOWDOWN

"Lieke is a gifted player who loves to dribble and beat players in one-on-one situations. She can create chances from wide positions, or come inside to score herself."

··

bottom of their group. Two years later, however, it was a different story, when a young Netherlands team qualified for the World Cup finals for the first time. In their opening match, Lieke scored the team's first World Cup goal against New Zealand. The Netherlands were knocked out by finalists Japan, but their progress had been clear and their confidence growing.

Two years later, the Netherlands hosted the UEFA Euro 2017 tournament. In their first match against Norway in Utrecht, the team entered the stadium to kick off their campaign, and were met by an incredible sea of orange – orange shirts, orange flags, orange scarves. They won the group and advanced to the final with some strong results along the way. Facing rivals Denmark in the decider, Lieke and her team felt as though they were unbeatable. They won the match 4–2, with Lieke scoring the team's second goal. In front of a home crowd and with more than 28,000 fans,

Played for
SC
HEERENVEEN
VROUWEN
2009–10

Played for
VVV-
VENLO
2010–11

Played for
STANDARD
LIÈGE
2011–2012
Trophies:
*1 x Belgian/
Netherlands Super Cup*

Played for
DUISBURG
2012–14

the Netherlands claimed their first title. Lieke was named the player of the tournament. Every sacrifice she had ever made had been worth it.

MAJOR MOVE

Following the tournament, Lieke moved from Swedish club FC Rosengård, where she had formed a deadly strike partnership with legend Marta, to European giants Barcelona. After scoring 20 goals in 28 games for Rosengård, many of Europe's top clubs were interested in the forward, but it was an easy decision for Lieke – she chose the Catalan club she had supported growing up.

By the age of 24, she was playing for the same club as her childhood hero, Brazil legend Ronaldinho, had done. It was a dream come true. Having already been named UEFA Player of the Year for 2017, in September FIFA announced the nominees for the Best Player in the World. Lieke shared a private plane with Barcelona clubmate Lionel Messi to the ceremony in London and returned with the trophy.

POSTER GIRL

Lieke and her Netherlands Euro 2017-winning teammates completely changed how people in the Netherlands viewed women's football. They captured the imagination of the country. Each of their matches in the tournament was a sell-out and the final was watched by a Dutch TV audience of 4.1 million – a quarter of the population.

The team built on their success by qualifying for their second World Cup in France 2019, beating Switzerland over two legs in the European play-off. With a mix of youth and experience, the Netherlands headed to the tournament full of belief, and they didn't disappoint. Despite playing with a

Played for
KOPPARBERGS/
GÖTEBORG
2014–15

Played for
FC ROSENGÅRD
2016–17
Trophies: *1 x Swedish Cup,*
1 x Swedish Super Cup
Teammates: *Marta*

UEFA
Women's Championship:
Winner 2017

The Best FIFA
Women's Player:
Winner 2017

toe injury, Lieke and her goals helped her side go all the way to the final – their best ever performance at a World Cup. The Netherlands were finally undone by a strong Unites States side, but proudly claimed the silver medal.

Lieke is keen to inspire more girls to take up the game and follow their dreams by showing them that a girl from a small village in the Netherlands can win the Euros and play for Barcelona. Now, instead of Ronaldinho,

Messi and co., it is Martens or Miedema that appear on the back of young fans' shirts. Lieke couldn't be prouder.

FUTURE GOALS

As ever, Lieke continues to dream big. The forward's next goals are to win the Spanish league with Barcelona and to help the Netherlands to make their Olympic debut at the 2020 Olympics in Tokyo. Lieke will undoubtedly be leading from the front.

KEY SKILLS

CLINICAL FINISHING

INCREDIBLE SPEED

TOP TECHNIQUE

UEFA Women's Player of the Year: Winner 2017

UEFA Women's EURO 2017: Player of the Tournament

Played for
FC BARCELONA
2017–present
Trophies: *1 x Spanish Cup*
Teammates: *Claudia Pina, Caroline Graham Hansen*

Shortlisted for the Ballon d'Or Féminin: 2018

2019 FIFA Women's World Cup: Runner-up

"I was told women couldn't play football. Now I can laugh."

LIEKE MARTENS

ADA HEGERBERG

DREAMING BIG

In 2018, stellar striker Ada Hegerberg became the first female winner of the Ballon d'Or, an annual prize to honour football's greatest players.

The girl from a tiny town in the middle of Norway never imagined she would become a professional footballer, believing she would have to get a 'real job' when she grew up. Fast-forward to the present day and Ada has already achieved so much in the game; at the age of 23, the number of trophies she had won had hit double figures. Her commitment to standing up for equal opportunities for women has won her many fans in the football community and beyond.

FORWARD

STATS

Country	Norway
Club	Olympique Lyonnais
Born	10 July 1995
Height	1.76 m
Club appearances	247
Club goals	281
International caps	66
International goals	38

HEGERBERG
14

FOOTBALL FAMILY

Ada grew up as part of a real footballing family. Both her mother and father were coaches and her elder sister not only played in a boys' team, she was the captain. In those early days, it was her sister, Andrine, who was the superstar, until Ada fell in love with football at around the age of 11. In Sunndalsøra her small, rural town of 7,000 people, Ada did not experience the same prejudices that some of her peers faced when starting out – everyone was equal. Ada had the talent, but talent alone would not take her to the top.

In 2007, the family moved to Kolbotn, where the sisters played together in

Norway's premier women's league, Toppserien. While still 16 years old, Ada finished as Kolbotn's top scorer in her first season and was voted the league's Young Player of the Year. The following campaign, the sisters moved on to Stabæk IF, a club near the Norwegian capital, and again, Ada became the division's leading goalscorer, with an impressive 25 goals in 18 matches.

At the age of 17, Ada had the chance to play abroad in eastern Germany with Turbine Potsdam. This meant leaving her family and striking out on her own. The schedule was gruelling, training three times a day, often in the snow or freezing rain, all while trying to keep up with her schoolwork. She would go home each night aching and exhausted,

More than 1 billion television viewers worldwide watched the FIFA Women's World Cup held in France in 2019.

CASEY'S LOWDOWN

"Strong, quick and direct, Ada can score tremendous goals with both her feet and her head. Who knows how far Norway might have gone with Ada in their World Cup 2019 squad?"

but would never complain. Ada knew that to play at the highest level she was going to be tested, pushed to her limits.

FRENCH EVOLUTION

In 2014, Ada was offered a contract with a giant of women's football and she jumped at the chance. Olympique Lyonnais Féminin had twice won the UEFA Champions League and were dominant in the French league. This was a world-class club that treated its women's and men's teams with equal respect, something that Ada values above all else. In Lyon, Ada had found a club that matched her own desire to win – and with style.

Ada's 26 goals in 22 league games in her debut season helped Lyon to win their ninth

Played for
KOLBOTN FOTBALL
2010–11
Teammate: *Andrine Hegerberg*

Played for
STABÆK IF
2012–13
Trophies: *1 x Norwegian Cup*

Played for
FFC TURBINE POTSDAM
2013–2014

league title in a row, while her strike in the French cup final secured the double.

The following campaign was even more special: this time, a treble of trophies – the French League cup and the Champions League – all belonged to Lyon. Ada's performances and incredible goals tally were at the heart of the club's success. A jaw-dropping 54 goals in 35 games saw the young striker honoured as the UEFA Women's Player of the Year. At 23 years old, she was quite simply unstoppable.

Lyon retained both the league and Champions League trophies for two more seasons, with Ada's talent continuing to shine. The world was watching. Then, one morning in 2018, Ada's coach called her into his office after training. He had a secret. Ada was going to be awarded the Ballon d'Or Féminin, the first time that a women's player had ever received the coveted prize.

SPECIAL NIGHT

The Ballon d'Or ceremony was an incredible night for Ada. Six more of her teammates from Lyon had been nominated for the award, but only one player could win. Even when the host of the awards made a sexist joke, Ada was determined not to let it take the shine off the evening. She was surrounded by love and respect in a room full of football legends. Heroes of the men's game such as Luka Modric and Kylian Mbappé knew exactly the hard work and sacrifices that Ada had made – the highs and heartaches are the same for men and women. That night, Ada became a legend.

NORWAY'S LOSS

Hegerberg also achieved great things on the international stage early in her career. She made her senior debut for Norway as a 17-year-old, and was selected

Played for
OLYMPIQUE LYONNAIS
2014 – present
Trophies: *4 x UEFA Champions League Titles,*
5 x French League Titles, 4 x French Cups
Teammates: *Wendie Renard,*
Saki Kumagai, Amandine Henry

2016 UEFA
Women's Player
of the Year Award:
Winner

2017 BBC
Women's Footballer
of the Year:
Winner

2018 Ballon
d'Or Féminin:
Winner

Shortlisted for
the BBC Women's
Footballer of the
Year: 2019

"You can't let anybody take your fire away from you. If you have big dreams, the fire is the only thing that will get you there."

ADA HEGERBERG

in the Norwegian squad for the 2013 UEFA Women's Championship, as the Grasshoppers reached the final. Her five goals at the 2015 World Cup in Canada earned her a nomination for the Best Young Player Award and the Norwegian Gold Ball award that year – the first time a woman had won the award in 20 years.

Following the team's early exit from the 2017 UEFA Women's Championship, though, Ada announced she would be taking a break from international football. Frustrated at the lack of opportunities being offered to girls in her home country, the striker has not returned to international duty since. The fact that she is prepared to miss out on playing in some of the biggest tournaments in women's football in the hope that future generations of girls will have better conditions says much about Ada's extraordinary character. While Norway competed at the Women's World Cup 2019 without their brightest star, Ada's focus remained purely on her desire to improve her game at Lyon.

Still only aged 24, years of devastating defences lie ahead of her. The sign of a true champion is to keep on winning, and Ada is just as hungry for success now as she was a decade ago. Her next challenge is to overtake German striker Anja Mittag and become the record scorer in the UEFA Champions League. Just a handful of goals shy of her target, few would bet against Ada Hegerberg, the golden girl from Sunndalsøra.

MORE AMAZING PLAYERS

AMANDINE HENRY

28 September 1989	France
Midfielder	International caps: 88
Olympique Lyonnais	International goals: 13

One of the world's greatest defensive midfielders, Amandine's composure on the ball and excellent range of passing have won her many fans, as well as the captain's armband for France. She was awarded the Silver Ball for the second-best player at the 2015 World Cup. Most of the midfielder's career to date has been in French football, though a move to the Portland Thorns in 2016 saw her become a NWSL champion. Amandine is now in her second spell at Lyon, where she has won an incredible 11 league titles and the Champions League five times. France's best player at the 2019 World Cup, Amandine has ambitions to win a title with *Les Bleues*.

Free-scoring midfielder/forward Lindsey skipped college football in the US to sign a six-figure deal with Paris Saint-Germain (PSG), at the age of 18. She stayed with PSG for four seasons, scoring 46 goals in 58 appearances. Lindsey signed for current club Portland Thorns in 2016, where she plays as a central midfielder – the same role as for her national side. In 2018, she was named the Most Valuable Player for the NWSL. She has won more than 70 caps and contributed 10 goals for the US, and was a key player at the 2019 World Cup, scoring twice as the US were crowned champions. Lindsey was shortlisted for the BBC's Women's Footballer of the Year 2019.

LINDSEY HORAN

26 May 1994	United States
Forward & Midfielder	International caps: 74
Portland Thorns	International goals: 10

STEPH HOUGHTON

23 April 1988	England
Defender	International caps: 112
Manchester City	International goals: 13

HOUGHTON
5

England and Manchester City captain Steph leads by example in the heart of defence, and is a role model for young players everywhere. She has played for the Lionesses at three World Cups and was selected for Team GB at the London 2012 Olympics. The versatile defender, who is strong at set pieces, has reached double figures for goals scored for both club and country. Thanks to her consistent displays, Steph won her 100th cap for England in November 2018, while at home has won a haul of trophies for Arsenal and Manchester City.

FRAN KIRBY

29 June 1993	England
Forward	International caps: 45
Chelsea	International goals: 13

KIRBY
10

Fran is a forward who loves to charge towards the goal with the ball at her feet. She can play on either wing as a classic number 10. She started out playing in an all-girls' side in a boys' league, where her dazzling play quickly earned the respect of her opponents. Fran began her career with Reading, before moving to Chelsea for what was then a British-record transfer fee for a women's player. Fran was in the England squad that finished third at the 2015 World Cup and scored a fine solo goal in the bronze-medal play-off against Sweden at France 2019. Dubbed a 'mini Messi', she was shortlisted alongside fellow Lioness Lucy Bronze for the 2018 Ballon d'Or award, a prize that one day could undoubtedly bear Fran's name.

EUGÉNIE LE SOMMER

18 May 1989
Forward
Olympique Lyonnais

France
International caps: 164
International goals: 76

Eugénie took up the sport at the tender age of two, and began playing against boys from the age of four until she was 14. She was also talented at judo, but her first love – football – won out. Eugénie made her international debut for *Les Bleues* at the age of 19, and moved to French and European champions Lyon the following year. As one of the smaller players in women's football, Eugénie is fast and creative, with a hunger to score goals – averaging almost a goal a game for her club. Incredible!

ALMUTH SCHULT

9 February 1991
Goalkeeper
VfL Wolfsburg

Germany
International caps: 64

Athletic keeper Almuth made her debut for Germany aged 21, the young stopper taking over the number-one jersey from German legend Nadine Angerer. Her excellent aerial ability and commanding presence in her box helped lead Germany to Olympic glory in 2016, as Almuth played every minute of the tournament. France 2019 was the keeper's first World Cup. Almuth plays her club football in Germany for Wolfsburg, where she has won the Bundesliga title twice as well as the Champions League.

DZSENIFER MAROZSÁN

18 April 1992
Midfielder
Olympique Lyonnais

Germany
International caps: 92
International goals: 32

In 2007, Dzsenifer made history by becoming the Bundesliga's youngest female player at just 14. From a footballing family, her father, Janos, played for Hungary, though Dzsenifer chose to represent Germany, the country in which she grew up and which she now captains. The midfielder's highlight with the national side was scoring in the final of the Olympics in Rio in 2016 to secure the gold medal for Germany. Dzsenifer plays her club football for European giants Lyon and has won League and Champions League titles three seasons in a row during her time there. Injury sadly cut short her 2019 World Cup campaign.

Vivianne's first memory of football is when she lost two teeth in a collision with a goalkeeper at the age of five – an incident that did nothing to put her off! The flying forward grew up playing against boys until she was 14, when she was offered her first professional contract with SC Heerenveen. Her national team debut came aged 17, and Vivianne has since scored a jaw-dropping 61 goals in 82 international appearances. In 2017, her goals in the semi-final, and double in the final, helped the Netherlands win their first women's Euro on home soil. Vivianne scored three times at the World Cup in France in 2019, having broken the record for WSL goals in a single season with English club Arsenal earlier in the year.

VIVIANNE MIEDEMA

15 July 1996	Netherlands
Forward	International caps: 82
Arsenal	International goals: 61

MIEDEMA
9

JORDAN NOBBS

18 December 1992	England
Midfielder	International caps: 56
Arsenal	International goals: 7

NOBBS
4

Roving midfielder Jordan is England's vice-captain, and has won more than 50 caps for her country. Her excellent ball control, work rate and assists record has helped her win a host of trophies with Arsenal during a nine-year spell with the club. Jordan made her England debut aged 19 and was a member of the Lionesses squad that finished third at the 2015 Women's World Cup in Canada. She was unfortunate to miss out on the 2019 World Cup through injury, but remains a first-choice Lioness when fully fit.

MEGAN RAPINOE

5 July 1985	United States
Midfielder	International caps: 158
Seattle Reign	International goals: 50

RAPINOE
15

Midfielder Megan is one of the United States' most important players, and has helped the country to win an Olympic gold medal at London 2012 and two World Cups, in 2015 and 2019. She can score goals, provide assists for teammates and shoot with both feet. Her six goals and three assists for the World Champions earned her both the Golden Ball and Golden Boot trophies at France 2019. Now in her mid-thirties, Megan remains a driving force in midfield for her country and domestic club, the Seattle Reign.

RISING STARS

SALMA BACHA

9 November 2000
Defender
Olympique Lyonnais

France U-20
International caps: 12
International goals: 8

Dynamic defender Selma combines playing in a star-studded side at Lyon with her studies in science and technology. She won the French League title and the UEFA Champions League with her club when she was only 17. Selma is hoping to break into France's senior side very soon.

KADEISHA BUCHANAN

5 November 1995
Defender
Olympique Lyonnais

Canada
International caps: 92
International goals: 4

Kadeisha burst onto the global stage representing Canada at the 2015 World Cup, where she picked up the award for the Best Young Player. She's the anchor in the centre of Canada's defence and has already won a host of trophies with her club side, Lyon, including a hat-trick of Champions League crowns.

ELLIE CARPENTER

28 April 2000
Defender
Portland Thorns

Australia
International caps: 39
International goals: 1

Defender Ellie moved continents from Australia to the USA to follow her dream when she was 17. Now with Portland Thorns, her teammates include Christine Sinclair, Lindsey Horan and fellow Aussie Caitlin Foord. Ellie is the NWSL's youngest scorer – scoring just weeks after her 18th birthday. She is a regular international for Australia's senior squad, too.

These 12 starlets are among the brightest young players in the world, with the talent to take them to the top. They are all performing beyond their years for their clubs. Some are already making headlines with their national sides, too. Remember their names.

DEYNA CASTELLANOS

18 April 1999
Forward
Florida State Seminoles

Venezuela
International caps: 13
International goals: 6

Deyna is a striker with a fantastic scoring record. She plays club football for American college side Florida State University and was nominated for the Best FIFA Women's Player award in 2017, aged 18, despite never having played professionally. She made her first appearance for Venezuela in the 2018 Copa América Femenina, marking her debut with a goal.

LAUREN HEMP

7 August 2000
Forward
Manchester City

England U-20
International caps: 6
International goals: 3

Manchester City's free-scoring young forward is one of the hottest prospects in English football. Her goal in the 2019 FA Cup final helped the Sky Blues lift the trophy. She was named England Young Player of the Year in 2017 and PFA Women's Young Player of the Year in 2018. That same year, Lauren helped England to a third-place finish at the 2018 FIFA U-20 Women's World Cup.

JORDYN HUITEMA

8 May 2001
Forward
Paris Saint-Germain

Canada
International caps: 23
International goals: 6

Tall teen striker Jordyn is one of the most exciting prospects in Canadian football. She made her national team debut for Canada at the age of 15 and scored six goals in her first 23 senior appearances. Jordyn had to wait until she turned 18 before signing her first pro contract, and chose French giants Paris Saint-Germain, having previously made a couple of guest appearances for the club.

The youngest player ever to feature in a World Cup final was Germany's Birgit Prinz – 17 years, 236 days old in the 1995 final.

LAUREN JAMES

16 April 2002
Forward
Manchester United

England U-19
International caps: 4

Lauren comes from a talented footballing family – her dad is a coach and her brother Reece is on the books at Chelsea. The forward kicked off her senior career with Arsenal, but followed Casey Stoney to Manchester United for their first season in the FA Women's Championship. She scored twice for the Red Devils in their opening league fixture and helped the team to clinch the league title.

CLAUDIA PINA

12 August 2001
Forward
Barcelona Femení

Spain U-20
International caps: 5
International goals: 1

Claudia joined Barcelona's U12 team and rose up the ranks to make her senior debut when she was just 16 – Barça's youngest female player. She began her career playing *futsal*, a game played on a hard, smaller pitch, and is showing great promise as a two-footed striker who has scored some incredible goals. The focused forward dreams of a call-up to Spain's senior squad one day.

MALLORY PUGH

29 April 1998
Forward
Washington Spirit

United States
International caps: 59
International goals: 18

Mallory 'Mal' Pugh is a flying forward who can score with both feet. She plays her club football for Washington alongside Marta and Sam Kerr, and has managed to notch up over 50 caps with World Champions the USA. Mal made her debut as a 17-year-old and played at the Rio Olympics in 2016. She was a member of the United States' World Cup-winning squad in 2019.

LEA SCHÜLLER

12 November 1997
Forward
SGS Essen

Germany
International caps: 17
International goals: 9

Lea made an outstanding start to her international career, leading the line with eight goals in her first 12 matches for Germany. With great technical and aerial abilities, Lea would love to emulate Germany's great striker Birgit Prinz in the future. She plays her domestic football in the German League for SGS Essen. She made her World Cup debut at France 2019 against China and scored against Nigeria.

KHADIJA SHAW

31 January 1997
Forward
Girondins de Bordeaux

Jamaica
International caps: 29
International goals: 31

Another of the Reggae Girlz' fine young players, Khadija was the leading scorer in the entire world during World Cup qualifying for France 2019! An incredible haul of 19 goals in 12 matches helped Jamaica qualify for the tournament for the first time. Khadija plays her club football for Girondins de Bordeaux and has escaped gang violence, that saw three of her brothers killed, to follow her dream.

GEORGIA STANWAY

3 January 1999
Forward
Manchester City FC

England
International caps: 12
International goals: 1

Named the PFA Women's Young Player of the Year in 2019, fearless forward Georgia is making a name for herself as one of the brightest young talents in England. Known for her stunning, long-range strikes, she's a regular starter for Manchester City. Georgia impressed as the youngest member of England's World Cup squad that reached the semi-finals in 2019.

MORE GREAT GAME-CHANGERS

DR RIMLA AKHTAR

FOOTBALL ASSOCIATION EXECUTIVE

Rimla is one of the most influential women in sport. She sits on several boards and is the first Muslim woman on the FA Council in England, an organization that is underrepresented by both women and people of colour. Rimla also chairs the Muslim Women's Sport Foundation, working to raise awareness and provide sporting opportunities for women, in particular those from ethnic minority communities. The child of Pakistani immigrants, who has been wearing a hijab since she was 11, Rimla herself experienced discrimination from a young age. Rimla has also received an MBE for her outstanding contribution to equality and diversity.

BARONESS KARREN BRADY

FOOTBALL CLUB CHIEF EXECUTIVE

British multimillionaire businesswoman Karren has worked in English football for three decades and is known as the 'first lady of football'. She became a director of a major publishing company, Sport Newspapers Ltd, at just 20, and a managing director of Birmingham City Football Club aged 23, at a time when it was unheard of for women to work in such roles in football. She has enjoyed a successful career in business and as a TV personality, and is the current chief executive of Premier League club West Ham United FC. Karren became a Baroness in 2014 and works in the House of Lords in London.

Heroes aren't only made on the pitch – women in a number of roles in football continue to stand up for equality in the game, making strides so that future generations of women and girls can enjoy the sport they love. While there is still work to be done to raise the profile of women's football, these pioneers have bravely broken barriers in a traditionally male world, challenging stereotypes and inspiring others. Here are the stories of just a few of these women, in celebration of their achievements.

MARINA GRANOVSKAIA

FOOTBALL CLUB CHIEF EXECUTIVE

Russian-Canadian Marina has earned herself a reputation as one of the most powerful women in football, acting as billionaire owner Roman Abramovich's representative at Chelsea FC. The formidable club chief executive is in charge of transfers for both the men's and women's squads, as well as the hiring and firing of managers. When a new star signs for the Blues, it is Marina who presents the player to the media, rather than the team's coach. She is said to be a tough negotiator when it comes to buying and selling players and renewing their contracts, earning her the nickname the 'Iron Lady'.

FATIM JAWARA

FORMER PLAYER AND REFUGEE

Promising goalkeeper Fatim Jawara played for the Red Scorpions in the Gambia and made her debut for the national women's football team aged 18. The teenager was determined to follow her dream to become a professional footballer, so her agent paid for her to board a hazardous sea crossing to Europe, along with other African migrants, in 2016. Tragically, the boat sank when hit by a sudden storm and Fatim did not survive. Her friends told reporters that Fatim knew the risks, but 'just loved the game so much'.

ANNA KESSEL

SPORTS JOURNALIST

In an industry dominated by men, Anna is a rare female sports journalist, as well as an author and tireless campaigner for equality in sport. She co-founded Women in Football (WiF), an organization that champions female role models while tackling the issue of sexism in the game. She has used her respected journalistic skills to cover three Olympic Games, several World Cups, Euros and World Championships, and interviewed some of the biggest stars in global sport.

NADIA NADIM

DENMARK INTERNATIONAL AND REFUGEE

Nadia was born in Afghanistan, where playing football in public was illegal. When she was just 10 years old, Nadia's father was killed by the Taliban, an army of extreme fighters who controlled the country at the time. Nadia and her family were forced to flee her war-torn home and, after travelling across Europe, they ended up in a refugee camp in Denmark. Here, she could play football freely. Her career progressed in Denmark and Nadia was awarded the captain's armband for her adopted country in 2009. The energetic forward has since played for some of the top clubs in the United States, England and France.

More than 200 broadcasters attended the 2019 World Cup, many giving games prime-time slots on network television.

JACQUI OATLEY BROADCASTER

Growing up, Jacqui didn't think that it was an option for women like her to work in football, but she was ready to change the game. She played amateur football for Chiswick Ladies until ruptured knee ligaments ended her playing career. Jacqui studied journalism and joined BBC Radio Leeds as a sports reporter. Her big break came in 2015 when she began commentating on the BBC's flagship TV programme *Match of the Day*, becoming the show's first female commentator. Jacqui has championed women working in football throughout her career but believes the sport is still 'a couple of generations away' from being a level playing field. She was awarded an MBE for her contribution to sports broadcasting in 2016.

HOPE POWELL COACH AND FORMER PLAYER

Hope started out playing on the streets of London with her brothers. She made headlines when FA rules banned her from representing her school team beyond the age of 11. That same year, she joined Millwall Lionesses, where she spent a large part of her career as a goal-scoring midfielder. Hope played for England 66 times before being appointed the first full-time coach of the national team, aged 31. She was the first woman and the first non-white person to land any top job within the English national football set-up. In 2011, England reached the quarter-finals of the Women's World Cup under Hope. She spearheaded the provision of contracts for her players, so women were paid to play for the first time, and she fought hard to establish the Women's Super League, which kicked off in 2011.

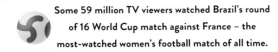

Some 59 million TV viewers watched Brazil's round of 16 World Cup match against France – the most-watched women's football match of all time.

FATMA SAMOURA

FOOTBALL EXECUTIVE

Senegalese diplomat Fatma was the first woman to become general secretary for the world football's governing body FIFA, and the first woman to sit on FIFA's board since it was founded 100 years ago. Her job is to manage the organization's finances and international relations, as well as to help plan the World Cup tournaments. Before joining FIFA, Fatma worked for the UN's world food programme, which delivers food to people affected by civil war, drought and famine. She is not afraid to stand up for equality, no matter how powerful her opponents may be.

RACHEL YANKEY

COACH AND FORMER PLAYER

Women's football was still developing when Rachel was growing up and there were few girls' teams. She pretended to be a boy – calling herself 'Ray' – for her first club and shaved her head to look the part. When she switched to a girls' team, Rachel had to overcome horrible comments from parents of other players to follow her goal. In 2000, when Rachel was 20, she became the first professional women's player in England, moving from Arsenal to Fulham. When her contract ended, Rachel coached young footballers. An awesome attacker, Rachel won six Premier League titles and nine FA Cups with Arsenal, and in 2012 became the most-capped England player, male or female.

122

> **"Never give up - there will be ups and downs and it's not an easy ride, but believe in yourself and you can make it."**

ALEX SCOTT — FOOTBALL JOURNALIST AND FORMER PLAYER

Alex Scott MBE grew up on a council estate in London's east end and fell in love with football at a young age. She signed for Arsenal's Academy aged eight, winning the English league title six times, as well as the Champions League and seven FA cups. She played 140 times for England. After hanging up her boots aged 33, Alex became the first female football pundit that the BBC had taken to a men's World Cup. Now a full-time TV presenter, Alex's in-depth knowledge and sharp analysis of the game has won her many supporters, though many have been quick to criticize. Determined to act as a positive role model, Alex hopes to open doors for other women to be taken seriously in football.

BIBIANA STEINHAUS — REFEREE

German referee Bibiana Steinhaus made Bundesliga history in 2017 when she became the league's first female referee of a men's game, in what was a real breakthrough for women in football in the country. An assured and experienced referee, Bibiana had previously taken charge of high-profile matches in women's football, including at two World Cups, the London 2012 Olympics and over seven seasons in the Women's Champions League.

CONCLUSION

Banned, discriminated against and paid little or nothing for their talents… these are just some of the challenges that have faced some of the greatest players in the women's game for 100 years. But women are strong and make fierce competitors. With each generation, their determination, hard work and talent have broken down barriers the world over, paving the way for a bright future of women's football.

When I began my career, I couldn't even dream of playing and coaching professionally, in front of packed stadiums and with TV cameras filming our games, because none of this was even possible. But the game has been slowly changing, the dreams are real and I'm excited for the future of women's football. Now, more girls and women all over the world are getting the opportunities to play the game they love, with freedom.

If the stories of these pioneering women have inspired you, believe in yourself, reach for the stars, and get behind your team. We all know that little girl who started with a dream. Do it for her!

Casey Stoney, MBE

INDEX

BIBLIOGRAPHY

Many articles, interviews, podcasts, websites and books – in many different languages – were pored over in the writing of this book.

If you're interested in learning more about the women's game, here are just some of the sources to help you begin your footballing journey.

MAGAZINES
France Football
She Kicks

BOOKS
In a League of their Own: The Dick, Kerr Ladies
  by Gail J Newsham (Paragon Publishing, 2018)
The Dick, Kerr Ladies
  by Barbara Jacobs (Robinson, 2004)

WEBSITES
• arsenal.com/women
• bbc.co.uk/sport/football/womens
• fcbarcelona.com/en/football/womens-football/news
• fifa.com/womens-football
• mancity.com/news/mcwfc
• manutd.com/en/news/women
• ol.fr/en/women
• olympic.org
• shekicks.net
• thefa.com/womens-girls-football
• theguardian.com/football/womensfootball
• theplayerstribune.com
• uefa.com/women
• ussoccer.com
• women.liverpoolfc.com
• womeninfootball.com

ACKNOWLEDGEMENTS

Firstly a massive thank you to my family for always supporting me throughout my career, from playing to coaching, and now management. To Megs, Teddy, Tilly and Willow – you are my motivation and inspiration. Love you all.

So much love and thanks to Terry Byrne and the team at 10Ten Talent, including Tom Caplan, Terry Ellis and David Shevel. What a journey we have been on together. Your support means the world to me.

Perminder Mann, thank you for believing in this project and being such an inspirational force for women in business. To Sophie Blackman, Emily Stead, Violet Tobacco, Rob Ward and all at Studio Press for all your hard work. I really appreciate your efforts.

Finally, to all of the amazing women featured in the book – and even those who are not – who relentlessly drive the women's game forward and are inspiring the next generation to dream big.